FAMILY RULES OKAY

MATT HUDSON

To my grandson Leo, World War II is where this work began, and it is here in World War III that it has come to fruition. You will not believe how people behaved and called it 'normal', how families were targeted by corporation-led government systems to break them down and enslave the broken individuals that were left. You won't believe me because by the time you're old enough, the war will have ended, and we will be free. Your grandfather, like my grandfather, was on the right side of history.

Foreword

Family Rules give us the foundations to 'rise and shine.' Matt Hudson's book is packed full of easy to read, plain speaking explanations of the importance of our families. Matt brings us on the journey with him as we wander together, discovering *Family Rules* that act as gatekeepers, preventing us from living our best life. They are the surface words that activate deeper psychological and physiological processes which must be obeyed or else!

This book explains in a down to earth way, how our minds work. He gives many examples that piece together the social fabric of the individual, the family and society as a whole. Matt's theory of 'Split-second Unlearning' clearly demonstrates the speed at which intense emotional experiences can control and influence our lives in the future. His academic work reveals first time learning to be lifetime learning. We do not, however, have to be children in order for Split-second Learning to take place. Any event that is promoted as 'unprecedented' or 'novel' will have the same impact whether you are young or old; Fear does not discriminate!

The UK government and governments worldwide have been hypnotising us without our consent for years. They've sold the idea to others, particularly in the last two years, where families have been exposed to fear, anxiety, and trauma. Matt uses mice studies to reveal the long-term effects of fear. These studies show the negative physical and mental impacts of trauma across 4 generations. This solution-based *Family Rules* book presents simple examples of evidenced explanations, it is an important resource for both individuals and families alike.

Notwithstanding the importance of the subjects discussed, *Family Rules* is full of humour and stories. It brings hope and solutions by enabling us to step into our Sovereignty and empowering us to say Enough! 'A sovereign man or woman will live a happier, healthier, longer life, and be in harmony with the planet'. Matt's insights are fundamental, profound and significant. Combined with the MindReset app, we have the potential to 'clear fear' creating a world where the family comes first.

Dolores Cahill
Professor

Acknowledgments

Where to begin thanking all of those who have contributed to this work in some way, shape or form? My grandparents, my grandfather for going to a war from which he and many others would not return. My grandmother lied to cover the pain of her loss and in doing so sowed the seeds of this book inside the mind of her grandson. To my parents, how on earth they managed to reach their seventies with the traumas they had experienced is beyond me; they could always find something to smile or be happy about, a secret that even science would support today.

Thank you to Plato, for showing us how the mind works in the most simplistic way, the shadows on the wall. The French physician and neurologist Hippolyte Bernheim in 1887 wrote "The evidence of facts will finally force itself upon the most skeptical minds and suggestive therapeutics, accepted and practiced by all physicians, will be one of the fairest conquests of contemporary medicine". Bernheim way back then had already proven the power of suggestion to conquer the ills of the mind and body. The torch that he held would light the way for Freud, Josef Breuer, Pierre Janet and on and on.

Thank you to Gregory Bateson who had the foresight to codify the therapeutic processes of Milton H. Erickson M.D., Fritz Perls M.D., and Virginia Satir Psychotherapist, into Neuro-linguistic Programming (NLP). Thank you to the creators of NLP, Richard Bandler and John Grinder whose process of modelling excellence continues to flourish in the fields of personal and business development. Thank you Wilf Proudfoot my first step into the mind began with you. Thank you Shelle Rose Charvet for *'Words That Change Minds'* and her amazing Language and Behaviour Profile work, which lead me to Patrick Merlevede for the inventory of attitude and motivation at work. This drove me to understand more of David McClelland's work around 'power' as a motivational driver.

Thank you to the psychiatrists Theodore Lidz and R.D Laing who believed, as did many of those I have studied, in a nonpharmacological solution to helping families, relationships and individuals to overcome psychophysiological 'dis-ease'. To this end, I would like to thank Professor Mark Johnson my co-author within the Split-second Unlearning Model for continuing to challenge my thoughts from an academic position.

Thank you to Henk Beljaars for your continued friendship and support through the darker days. To Andrew Zaranko, for daring to walk with me on the next stage of our journey to scientifically demonstrate the bridge between mind and body. To Michael Shane and Anthony Ancrum, our walks keep my feet on the ground. And to Lisa, thank you for having the capacity of grace to see beyond the here and now. You're helping to fuel my soul as well as supporting the work, so it reaches more who need it.

A special thank you to Professor Dolores Cahill whom we have followed closely for the last few years. A true hero in our eyes, who holds the doorway to freedom open for all who choose to rise. We are deeply humbled that you agreed to write the foreword for this book, there are no coincidences! The journey was intended to be about how subconscious Family Rules impact the lives of individuals within the family. However, the more I researched for the book, the further down the rabbit hole I went. This has resulted in the conclusion of Stockholm syndrome *en masse*, a *"folie en Société"*.

And thank you, dear reader, for being here at the start of our journey together, I can't wait to see who we are at the other end….

Contents

Introduction

"What did you say?" was a question I heard once too often from clients in a one-to-one therapeutic environment. Being conductively deaf from birth, I would find it particularly odd when my pace, tone and volume had not changed, yet the clients seemed to be unable to hear what I had just said.

I am eternally curious and I'm guessing that if you are reading this book, then you are too. Has it ever happened to you? You're sitting having a conversation with someone, you or they say something, and the words vanish? Usually, you will repeat the statement or adjust it a little and the conversation continues. However, since the client was paying for the interaction, I felt it better to have them go hunting for that which they had deleted. The point is, how and why were words subconsciously deleted?

My old mentor Wilf Proudfoot would encourage me to "let them struggle". These words would serve me well as I ventured forward into the world of personal development and coaching. There's a wonderful scene in *Harry Potter and the Philosopher's Stone*[1] where Harry, Hermione and Ron are caught in the Devil's Snare. This is a magical ivy that strangles its prey to death, the more you panic the tighter it squeezes. The spell to release you is relaxation! Remain calm and the

---

[1] J.K. Rowling.(1998) Harry-Potter-Philosopher's Stone

plant will let you go. As you can imagine, a plant such as this would claim many lives owing to the activation of the fight, flight, and freeze response system within the limbic system of the human brain. We will look at this later. The struggle that each of us faces at various points in our lives should have an end date, a point at which unlearning takes place to make room for the new. The problem is the mental health pandemic rages on without showing any signs of stopping. This drives me to wonder what the missing link is. How are we failing as a society to dispense with this affliction of the body and the mind?

The Saboteur Within-- The Definitive Guide to Overcoming Self Sabotage[2] was, for me, an attempt to bring long-term therapy to an abrupt halt by using NLP and un-hypnosis (a process of de-hypnotizing clients from unresourceful states of mind). However, there were still clients for whom following step by step guides to self-development just did not work!

Resourcefulness is all well and good when you are in it, but what prevents you from controlling your thoughts and stepping into the state of mind you want at the right time and place? I pondered for a long while about the possibility of a whole set of filters or mental programs that operate above meta programs[3], i.e., meta-meta-programs. These clients certainly fit some sort of pattern. They were generalizing, distorting and above all deleting what I was saying, and it appeared to be outside of their awareness. I decided to follow on from the work of Virginia Satir and look upon these patterns as 'Family Rules.' These are not to be mistaken for the rules that our parents or caregivers place upon us when we are children, to

---

[2] M. Hudson(2011) The Saboteur Within: The Definitive Guide To Overcoming Self Sabotage

[3] L.M. Hall &B.G. Bodenhamer (2003) The User's Manual for the Brain Volume II Mastering Systemic NLP

keep us safe from harm. They are the below conscious rules that create a conflict or threat response within the brains' stress system, causing a simultaneous reaction whenever anything remotely resembling the original context appears. Family Rules are therefore maladaptive mental programs that prevent us from reaching our full potential. Like meta programs, Family Rules run in specific contexts, however, unlike meta programs Family Rules are linked to direct survival, "I must obey, or I will die".

Now, on that cheery note, may I welcome you to Family Rules.

Matt Hudson

1
FAMILY RULES
THE BELOW CONSCIOUS STRUCTURE

"Vision is the art of seeing what
is invisible to others"
Jonathan Swift

Before we dive into Family Rules, I think it's best to give you some insights right at the beginning, which we can then use later as we examine the case studies.

Let me first introduce you to the American Psychiatrist Theodore Lidz (1910-2001), best known for his work on the causes of schizophrenia and how to help schizophrenic patients with psychotherapy. Lidz was an advocate for research into the environmental causes of mental illness and an ardent critic of the disproportionate focus on pharmaceutical treatments. Why are we beginning a book about Family Rules by talking about 'schizophrenia'? I hear you ask.

The etymology of *schizophrenia* is derived from the Greek *skhizein* 'to split' + *phrēn* 'mind' or 'heart'. In other words, a broken mind, or a broken heart. Lidz and his team looked at the environment where their patients were arriving from, the family home. He documented a high rate of psychological disturbances among the parents of schizophrenic children.

In their book *Schizophrenia and the Family* (1965), Lidz, fellow psychiatrist Stephen Fleck and Alice Cornelison assembled findings of what could be seen as the most detailed clinical study of a series of schizophrenic patients and their families. Their research group were interested in the communication that went on inside the family.

Lidz wrote:

> *"In [such] families the parents were rarely in overt disagreement, and the family settings were reasonably calm. But, as we studied these seemingly harmonious families, it became apparent that they provided a profoundly distorted and distorting milieu because one spouse passively acceded to the strange and even bizarre concepts of the more dominant spouse concerning child rearing and how a family should live together. We termed the seemingly harmonious ones as "skewed"."*[4]

If the overbearing influence of one of the parents went unchecked by the other then this, Lidz suggested, could lead to a phenomenon he called *folie à deux*, a shared delusion between both parents[5]. If, however, the delusional ideas of the dominant parent were allowed to flourish to all members of

[4] https://www.amazon.com/gp/product/082366001X
[5] Suresh Kumar PN, Subramanyam N, Thomas B, Abraham A, Kumar K. Folie à deux. Indian J Psychiatry. 2005 Jul;47(3):164-6. doi: 10.4103/0019-5545.55942. PMID: 20814461; PMCID: PMC2919794.

the family, a *folie en famille* would occur[6]. In other words, we have the foundation stones of Family Rules.

Our next building block for our exploration comes from the American psychotherapist Virginia Satir. In her book *'People Making'* Satir directs us to certain family rules that you live by, rules that you may be obeying without realizing. Satir was able to see through soft eyes and find love behind family miscommunication. The book was further updated to include extra chapters, which still stand the test of time. These include parent and child relations, self-worth, family systems, interpersonal relations, and a range of in-depth communication insights[7].

Virginia's work always left me with a warm fuzzy feeling. I have endeavoured to create this within all my client interactions. The search for greater self-worth, self-love and connection drives the process forward, always searching for the positive intention behind miscommunication or destructive behaviour.

I was fortunate enough to have trained with a dear friend of Virginia, Wilf Proudfoot, and it was Wilf who inspired me and thousands of other people to learn more about Satir's work. I owe him a debt of gratitude, he showed me how to maintain the client experience within a position of grace - A gentle, trusting, encouraging, supportive mindset that the coach or therapist must maintain. This will then become the resource state that the client will access outside of the session to engage the world.

If you have managed to grow up within a nurturing family then you will be among the very few, whose rules have been

---

[6] LIDZ RW, LIDZ T. The family environment of schizophrenic patients. Am J Psychiatry. 1949 Nov;106(5):332-45. doi: 10.1176/ajp.106.5.332. PMID: 18143863.

[7] Virginia Satir (1988) New People Making

updated as you grew. For most of us, however, we are still subconsciously obeying a command from long ago, so long in fact, that we can't even remember.

The Family Rules that we look at throughout this book will all have certain things in common. Let's begin with a brief overview of what you need to look out for when Family Rule hunting; or attempting to uncover if you, your partner, or your client are from *folie en famille*.

DELETION, DISTORTION AND GENERALISATION

Deletion

When you take in information, even though you don't realise it, you filter things immediately. Would you like to put this to the test? Before you read any further take 30 seconds and look around the room you are in for everything that is blue.

It can be any shade of blue. Now close your eyes and recall all the blue items you saw; I am sure you can recall a great many. Now, close your eyes again and recall everything you saw that was green. Nowhere near as many? Chances are you might not have noticed anything that is green, because you had your *'blue filter'* on whilst scanning the room. Your mind works in the same way.

If you need to find a certain book on a shelf, for example, you might 'delete' information you don't deem to be important, such as every other book on the shelf that isn't the book you need. You might begin by deleting the books that you know to be bigger than the book you need, then a particular shelf that you know doesn't include that book, etc.

You delete information because you don't need it at that point in time, not because it's not important. In a different context, the same data might be essential, and you might reprioritise everything to align with this. See how that works?

Distortion

One of the things that can get us into trouble is the way that we distort the information we take in. Now, this sounds like you're taking in information and making it different from what it is, but this isn't necessarily a bad thing.

For example, if you were to have the belief that the sky is red and someone else has the opinion that the sky is blue, you both feel you are right. You might each see the sky as the different colours you believe it to be.

So, you argue with the other person about what you see versus what they see. You both think you're right and you might both think the other person is wrong.

When you distort information, it's as though you're saying there is certain information that is right to you; you distort your own sense of reality. You might think something completely different to what another person says because you truly believe what you believe.

There's nothing inherently wrong with this process, everyone has their own experience of reality based on what they have experienced before, what they believe to be true and what they believe to be false. However, when you begin to say that only your experience is right, things can get a little tricky.

That's when people begin to argue. The way you distort things in your mind will change the way you view or feel about things. That in turn is based on the information you receive from the world around you.

Generalisation

When you take in new information, you might generalise that data based on what you have experienced in the past—this is when words such as 'always' and 'never' come into play. The brain believes that if you hurt your hand when you touched a hot kettle in the past, the same will happen the next time you touch a kettle. So, you might decide to be more careful when you're around kettles.

When a trainer trains a young elephant, it is tied with a rope to a peg in the ground. The young elephant truly believes that the rope and the peg are keeping it held in place.

He tries to pull on the rope and can't get free. The elephant learns to generalise his experience, so even as he grows bigger and stronger, he believes he will not be able to get free of the rope.

The generalisation of the belief causes elephants to 'always' feel they are captive when they are tied to a peg with the rope.

When we have certain experiences in life, we generalise them. That's how we make sense of them. We believe that each experience teaches us something about the future. Often we don't look outside of that experience.

Keeping these filters in mind when it comes to Family Rules allows you to see how children initially process information based on survival mechanisms and rules from parents/caregivers to keep the child safe. However, since they only have a limited set of experiences, it seems that children will have different outcomes for their thinking. This childlike perception can be maintained inside a Family Rule, which can lead to poor mental and physical health outcomes, deprivation and even a shorter life span[8].

COULD HAVE... WOULD HAVE... SHOULD HAVE... DIDN'T!!!

Many of us fall foul of the above words, knowing that you could have, but something stopped you. You would have but you thought someone else would too. You should have but you came up with a million reasons not to. I'm sure that this will feel familiar to you, often supported by self-talk, a voice inside your mind discouraging you, so that you fail to follow through on your desires, hopes and dreams.

---

[8] Finkelhor, D., Shattuck, A., Turner, H., and Hamby, S. (2015). A revised inventory of adverse childhood experiences. *Child Abuse Negl.* 48, 13–21. doi: 10.1016/j. chiabu.2015.07.011

The term used in linguistics to describe these words is "Modal Operators". Modal operators come in three forms necessity, possibility, and probability. When searching for a family rule, necessity is key.

Modal operator of Necessity will always come up in the shape of "Have to", "Should do", "Should have", "Must do", "Must have", "Shouldn't" or "Mustn't", "Ought to", "Need to".

If you run a few sentences through your mind about what you should do today or what you mustn't do, do you notice a feeling in the pit of your stomach? That's your alarm system alerting you to the rules that currently run your life.

Modal operators of Possibility words such as "can", "able to", "will", "want", "choose", "decide", "intend", on the other hand will ease the tension within your system and offer you ways forward. Simply by replacing the word should for could, can de-escalate or prevent an argument. "You can do this" feels a lot better than "You should do this", does it not?

Modal operators of Probability words such as "could", "would", "may", "might", add a dash of choice to your current thoughts, they are not definite, but they are probable.

MODALS AND THE VERBS THEY OPERATE BY

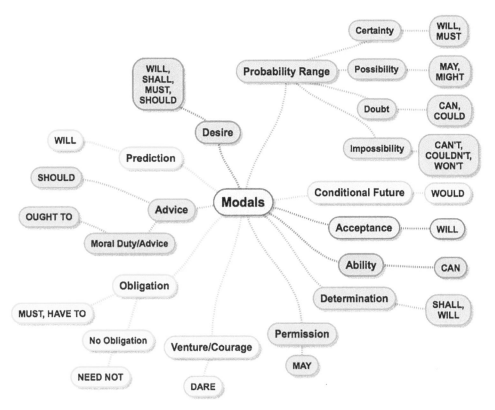

Adapted from www.eduvictors.com

AMNESIA

The amnesic state associated with Family Rules can also be found in cases of traumatic or violent events. Recent studies into brain imaging are beginning to shine light on the forgotten traumatic memories, as researchers seek a neurological signature that remains within the brain. "Trauma therapists assert that abuse experienced early in life can overwhelm the central nervous system, causing children to split off a painful memory from conscious awareness. They maintain that this psychological defence mechanism—known as dissociative amnesia—turns up routinely in the patients they encounter"[9].

Psychiatrist, Muriel Salmona[10], has written extensively on the subject of dissociative amnesia, so please check out her work. I find it fascinating how something traumatic can cause us to shut down and forget, when logically we might assume that, after surviving the experience, we would consciously remember every vivid detail. This is simply not the case.

It has long been known and studies have shown, almost all of us have suffered with some kind of adverse event during our childhood. Bessel van der Kolk[11] in his enlightening work around trauma and post-traumatic stress disorder (PTSD) suggests that psychological trauma may leave the victims with no conscious recollection of the traumatic experience, yet they could still express the imprint of the event through bodily expressions. These physiological changes can be validated via changes to the development of the brain as well as bodily expressions. Sadly, many of these victims, Van der Kolk tells us, are totally unaware of what they have lived through and

---

[9] Joshua Kendall (2021) https://www.scientificamerican.com/article/forgotten-memories-of-traumatic-events-get-some-backing-from-brain-imaging-studies/#:~:text=Trauma%20therapists%20assert%20that%20abuse,in%20the%20patients%20they%20encounter.

[10] Muriel Salmona (2018) https://www.memoiretraumatique.org/assets/files/v1/Articles-Dr-MSalmona/2018-Traumatic-Amnesia

[11] Van der Kolk, B. A. (1994). The body keeps the score: memory and the evolving psychobiology of posttraumatic stress. *Harv. Rev. Psychiatry* 1, 253–265. doi: 10.3109/10673229409017088

can give no verbal account[12]. Rothschild managed to sum it up succinctly: "The body remembers even if the mind cannot."[13]

One may begin to speculate what might happen to our children who have been in the traumatic grip of the Covid narrative for the past 2 years? We shall look further into this later.

SPLIT-SECOND UNLEARNING

You may be surprised to learn that all the above takes place within the blink of an eye. When a person feels threatened or experiences a traumatic event, real or imagined, their mind creates an emotional memory image (EMI) of the entire episode.

This mental image is then stored inside the mind's eye, at approximately arm's length and acts as an evolutionary survival mechanism. Whenever anything remotely similar to the original experience occurs, the EMI ignites the brains fight, flight, freeze response system. Think of it like a movement sensor on your house, when something is detected, the lights are activated. This works in virtually the same way.

The EMI is stored in the nonconscious mind, which prevents you from ever being able to consciously access or work with it. The repercussions of not clearing the emotional memory

---

[12] Van der Kolk, B. A., and Fisler, R. (1995). Dissociation and the fragmentary nature of traumatic memories: overview and exploratory study. *J. Trauma. Stress* 8, 505–525. doi: 10.1007/BF02102887

[13] Rothschild, B. (2000). *The Body Remembers: The Psychophysiology of Trauma and Trauma Treatment*. New York, NY: WW Norton & Company.

image can result in biological, neurological, physiological, behavioural or psychological problems[14].

If you were to think about why you are afraid of fire, you'll be able to come up with lots of logical reasons for being this way, all of them very wise and rational, but they don't answer the question - Why are you afraid? The genuine answer to the question is 'experience'. How did you gain your experience?

Prior to discovering that fire burns and causes pain, you would have been curious, intrigued and captivated by the bright colours emitting from the dancing flames. Perhaps, you were left unattended for a moment, and you seized your chance to learn…OUCH!!! A split-second was all it took for you to realize the flame is to be avoided for the rest of your life.

I know this may seem obvious, but if you pause for long enough and let this sink in, you might reach the realisation that I did. i.e., if you can learn something in a split-second then you can surely unlearn it. The challenge of course would be to uncover the original learning in order to upgrade or clear its psychophysiological imprint. To this end I hope that we can travel together to uncover the key to those unexplainable conditions, emotional outbursts, irrational behaviours, physical and *mental dis-ease*. Please note that my use of the word *dis-ease* is quite deliberate; the American Psychological Association define *mental disorder*:

> *Any condition characterized by cognitive and emotional disturbances, abnormal behaviours, impaired functioning, or any combination of these. Such disorders cannot be accounted for*

---

[14]   Matt Hudson & Mark I. Johnson. (2021) Split-Second Unlearning: Developing a Theory of Psychophysiological Dis-ease Frontiers in Psychology https://www.frontiersin.org/articles/10.3389/fpsyg.2021.716535

solely by environmental circumstances and may
involve physiological, genetic, chemical, social,
and other factors[15].

Hungarian-born Canadian endocrinologist Hans Selye (1907–1982) defined the ***disease of adaptation***:

> *any of a group of illnesses, including high blood*
> *pressure and heart attacks, that are associated*
> *with or partly caused by long-term defective*
> *physiological or psychological reactions to stress[16].*

As an educator who has spent 30 years studying the human mind, I propose the term **mental dis-ease,** as this removes the permanence that terms like disorder and disease convey. Dis-ease simply means an uneasiness or a lack of feeling at ease[17]. When we view our problems as symptoms of uneasiness then the next steps are to break free from the hypnotic spell that our past has cast upon us.

NON-VERBAL COMMUNICATION

The memories that relate to the presenting problem are stored within an EMI, as we've discovered. The below conscious response to a simple question will generate a pure, direct connection to the original experience. For example

> "What would you like to work with, right
> now, that would make the greatest difference
> to your life going forward?"

---

[15] https://dictionary.apa.org/mental-disorder
[16] https://dictionary.apa.org/disease-of-adaptation
[17] https://www.yourdictionary.com/dis-ease

Now, I wonder if you noticed that your eyes have just flicked to a certain position and back again. If you didn't that's okay, not many people realise the human eye makes 3 complete movements per second. These are called saccades. When it comes to diagnosing movement disorders, saccadic abnormalities are a key indicator specialists will look for[18]. But what if a build-up of cached memories is driving the problem? The thoughts (non-physical) impacting the physical body.

This scan is carried out nonconsciously, prior to formulating a conscious verbal reply. When a person encounters the troubling EMI, this triggers the negative somatic response, generating the non-verbal signals the therapist is looking for. While the conscious verbal answer may set the scene for psychotherapeutic exploration, their unconscious physical response indicates a distinct connection between a thought and a reflex—between mind and body.

You may observe tiny facial or bodily ticks, bodily asymmetry, maybe only one arm is moving whilst the person speaks. A sharp intake of breath, as the body's defence system takes in more oxygen in readiness for the onslaught from the invisible predator, who hides within the shadows of the mind. The face may appear momentarily childlike with a flush of white, (a snapshot of a frightened expression), as the body accesses the fear response, provoked by your seemingly harmless question.

Please keep in mind, if you are alive then the only requirement from your subconscious mind is that you repeat yesterday. Therefore, anyone who elects to sit in the therapeutic chair is very brave. They have put themselves forward for change,

[18] Termsarasab, P., Thammongkolchai, T., Rucker, J.C. *et al.* The diagnostic value of saccades in movement disorder patients: a practical guide and review. *J Clin Mov Disord* **2,** 14 (2015). https://doi.org/10.1186/s40734-015-0025-4

which goes against the engrained, automatic programs the mind has been running for years.

If we think about this from an energetic perspective, change costs more energy and more conscious effort, as the evolutionary parts of the brain continually attempt to enforce the known upon us.

A NOMINALISATION

Now, I don't mean to go all wordy on you, but you will need to get your head around this particular word if we are to work together here. A nominalisation is when we take an adjective (tells us more about the noun, for example, the large fish or red apple) or a verb (the action or state of being) and turn it into a noun. Specifically, the nominalisation 'freezes' the entire process within the mind's eye, which prevents the person from exiting the mental lockdown. The nominalisations are underlined in the following examples:

- I have some <u>admiration</u> for you. Instead of I admire you.
- Let me give you a better <u>explanation</u>. Instead of let me explain.
- Do these examples give you an <u>indication</u>? Instead of indicate, show, or prove how nominalisations work.

The nominalisations objectify and solidify the process; hence a lot of people use the word 'Stuck' when in therapy. In some way they feel that their life has become stagnant or unable to move. This can be the result of a psychological nominalisation

FAMILY LIKENESS

By Alison Jean Thomas

"You're just like them!" they say.
And me, I yell, "No way!
He's so moody,
She's so shrill,
His chin juts out,
Boy can she shout!
His nose is big,
And mine's quite small
There's no resemblance at all."

But then on days of harmony
I find that I agree.
Our family is made of different parts,
But we're all the same
In our hearts.

EXERCISE 1

Modal Operators – Necessity, Possibility and Probability

A Modal Operator sets the rules for the context 'before' we even know what the activity is. They are real game changers and can have huge neurological impacts on your client, family, friends. Remember the Family Rules sit within necessity, unless you were raised by Baloo the bear, the main fictional character featured in Rudyard Kipling's The Jungle Book, in which case you will look for the Bear-necessities, that's why a bear can rest at ease…[19]

Necessity $\longrightarrow$ **Nonnecessity**

> Words such as: should, have, must, need, supposed to, ought to

Possibility $\longrightarrow$ **Impossibility**

> Words such as: can, able to, will, want, choose, decide, Intend

Probability $\longrightarrow$ **Improbability**

> Words such as: could, would, may, might

---

[19] https://www.youtube.com/watch?v=6BH-Rxd-NBo Bear Necessities

Write down 3 examples from each category.

1.

2.

3.

CHAPTER SUMMARY

Family Rules are a set of filters that function alongside modal operators of necessity, possibility, probability, generalisations, deletions, and distortions. They are activated within a split-second and create the same below conscious reaction as the original experience. Although the reaction may seem spontaneous and current, it is in fact an automated re-enactment of the past, which is whirling round on a closed loop inside the mind of the client. The client will have no conscious recollection of the original event. Moving from impossibility to possibility and improbability to probability can open up new thought processes, which may transform your reality.

There are several other things to look out for on our journey together so in Chapter 2 we will use a map to act as our reference point.

2
THE MAP OF THE MIND

*"The world is a book, and those who
do not travel read only a page"*
Saint Augustine

As a young practitioner, I made my way from client to client, book to book, training to training, in search of the next technique, the next silver bullet that would transform the lives of my clients. "Jesus is back" was a phrase the family would use to describe my mental and physical state upon returning home from the latest mind-expanding training course. New information can nourish your soul and leave you hungry for more. It was after one of these journeys that I decided to plot a map to show how I believed the mind works. Yes, it sounds very arrogant, after all, who am I to come up with such a thing? Then I was reminded of the story of a little girl sitting in a classroom, busily drawing on a piece of paper. Her teacher inquired "What are you drawing?" The girl replied, "A picture of God, Miss". The teacher then spoke in disbelief "No one knows who God looks like." The girl, without looking up replied, "They will in a minute!" This little girl was and is my motivation, then and now.

As I sat listening to clients hour after hour, day after day, month after month, I began to see patterns developing in front of my eyes. The challenge was to capture them in a format or some kind of guide that would help me and eventually others, to track where the client may be stuck or trapped.

The classic NLP process is to take the client from the present state to the desired state. It was modelled on a mix of Satir, Milton Erickson and Fritz Perls' therapeutic approaches. NLP points to interference or miscommunication as being the barrier to a client reaching their goal. However, Family Rules are grounded in fear, not love.

Let me explain further. In order for a Family Rule to continue to run your life many years after it should have expired or been upgraded, it must operate on a below conscious level, and it must have been created with a large threat to your existence! Now, I'm not suggesting for one moment that your parents attempted to kill you, but a smaller, more vulnerable You, may have taken whatever happened and perceived it as life threatening. Here's an example:

You're 18 months old, sitting in the comfort of your play and curiously investigating a spider. It's something new and it's interesting. Suddenly, out of nowhere, your mother appears and seeing you're about to pop the spider in your mouth, screams "STOP!!!" at the top of her voice. Your stress response system is now scanning for a threat, it must be something huge as your main caregiver is freaking out! The only thing that is different within your safe zone is 'the spider,' therefore the next time and every time after this, you will run a mile rather than play with that cute little 8-legged friend you once knew.

This is how easily our minds can install threat responses; it only takes a split-second, as you now know. Fear is a multifaceted mechanism; when used in a short burst, can give us the extra energy to run that little bit faster or fight a little bit harder. From an evolutionary perspective, it's thanks to fear that we've managed to survive this long. As each of our ancestors attempted something for the first time, something different, they would pass on valuable information. When you think about it this way it makes sense as to why we may have an aversion to 'difference,' and why there may be family rules to guard us against this threat to our existence.

Fear is such a huge subject; a quick check on Google returns thousands of results and many specialists, so I won't be venturing too far into the subject in this book. I will, however, point to a few gems that I've picked up on my travels and share them with you.

In odour fear conditioning studies on mice[20] for instance, there were some fascinating results which were passed on to future generations. Science has noted that having a sensitivity to certain smells are built into our neurology and passed on epigenetically. These scents influence our ability to escape predators, identify good food, avoid harmful things, even play a part in our social bonding and who we choose as a mate. How cool is fear, right?

Well, Houston, we have a problem. Epidemiologists expected to see a DNA methylation mark within the olfactory receptor genes inside the brain, but they didn't. They so far have failed to explain how this learned fear is passed on from generation to generation. What's even spookier is *"not just the memory for the odour, but also the association of the odour with a fearful experience, is transmitted across generations."*

Now, scientists are baffled and are searching for some kind of *"communication mechanism"* which is *"as yet unknown"*. I particularly love the use of the word "transmitted" it has a kind of electrical resonance, radio waves and frequencies feel to it, don't you think? In fact, Professor Moshe Szyf from the Department of Pharmacology and Therapeutics, McGill University, Montreal, Quebec, Canada explained:

---

[20] Szyf, M. Lamarck revisited: epigenetic inheritance of ancestral odor fear conditioning. *Nat Neurosci* **17**, 2–4 (2014). https://doi.org/10.1038/nn.3603

"*...evolution has equipped organisms with mechanisms to respond specifically and efficiently to certain critical novel experiences, such as odour and predator threat, and to transmit this information effectively to their offspring with-out the need for the typically slow process of natural selection... An interesting question is whether there is a mechanism that could then fix these epigenetically driven phenotypic changes in the genetic sequence, thereby altering the course of evolution.*"

There's that "*transmit*" word again, perhaps the problem facing physical science is non-physical science! Edward O. Wilson, the pioneer of sociobiology and biodiversity, suggests:

"*a balanced perspective cannot be acquired by studying disciplines in pieces but through pursuit of the consilience among them*[21]."

Merriam-Webster defines consilience – "*the linking together of principles from different disciplines especially when forming a comprehensive theory*"[22]. Therefore, we had better keep this in mind as we tread further, I mean, just imagine what might happen to the course of human evolution if we were to view this physical, chemical problem through the lens of quantum science?

The theory of quantum entanglement establishes that even though two particles are separated they are still linked together in a certain way no matter how far apart they are in space. The 2022 Nobel prize in physics has just been awarded to Alain Aspect, John F. Clauser and Anton Zeilinger for their work in entangled photons. They've shown that information can be instantly transmitted over infinite distances, known as quantum

---

[21] Wilson, EO. (1999). *Consilience: The unity of knowledge* (Vol. 31): Vintage.
[22] https://www.merriam-webster.com/dictionary/consilience

teleportation[23]. These scientists are pioneering work into the field of informational science, yet if we apply consilience, are we not already proof of quantum entanglement?

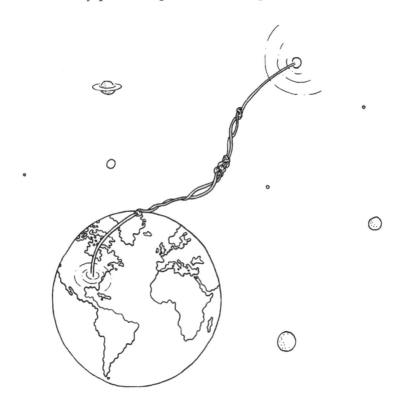

At a micro level the human body consists of approximately 37.2 trillion single cells[24], which are all held in place via an

[23] https://www.newscientist.com/article/2340852-no-bel-prize-in-physics-awarded-to-pioneers-of-quantum-infor-mation/?utm_source=nsday&utm_medium=email&utm_cam-paign=nsday_051022&utm_term=Newsletter%20NSDAY_Daily

[24] Eveleth, R. (2013, October 23). *There are 37.2 trillion cells in your body.* Smithsonian Magazine. Retrieved September 19, 2022, from https://www.smithsonianmag.com/smart-news/there-are-372-trillion-cells-in-your-body-4941473/

electromagnetic force at a subatomic level[25]. Therefore, you and I are more nothing than something. If the whole of you is subjected to a traumatic event in your past, that imprint could create a subatomic resonance pattern, which is continually being transmitted from that point in time to you, right now. The younger you is still afraid, caught up in the actual moment over and over, sending you the cry for help and asking what do we do about it? We try many ways to silence or put up with our 'problem.'

Maybe you're thinking the past has been holding onto you or maybe you have been holding onto your past? In the quantum field there is no past or future, only now. The family rule created back then continues to resonate from within you. It is like a fingerprint, a unique signature of yours marking time in space.

Speaking of marking time, let's march on and investigate our map. For those of you without military knowledge *'marking time'* means to march on the spot, left, right, left, right, moving nowhere left, right, left, right, burning up energy, left, right, left, right, awaiting further commands.

THE MAP OF THE MIND PROCESS

When introducing how I believe the mind works to an individual or a group, I begin with a blank piece of paper and add to it as I go along. I will use the same approach here so that you can model me and hopefully gain similar results.

---

[25] https://www.exploratorium.edu/origins/cern/ideas/standard2.html

THE BLANK PAGE

For many people the blank page can evoke fear, ask anyone who ever tried to write something meaningful or apply paint to a blank canvas. The nothing is where the wonders of the universe reside, all you have to do is begin. Consider what you're being asked to do when I say the word "draw"? The writer or the artist does not draw onto the blank page, they draw from the nothing onto the blank page.

The philosopher Immanuel Kant influenced my thoughts about the blank page with his metaphysical studies. In the *Critique of Pure Reason*[26] Kant shows us that there are limits to what we can know through theoretical reason, which he defines as the distinction between phenomena (objects as we experience them) and noumena (objects as they exist in themselves)[27].

The next time you face the blank page, pause for a moment, and consider what you are about to draw forth or draw out of the noumena so we may experience the phenomena. In the book *The Neverending Story*, by German writer Michael Ende,[28] 'The Nothing' is an invisible force that devours Fantastica. The actual antagonists are human beings, one by one they close their minds to fantasy and magical things, the result of which leaves nothing but a void. The Fantasticans who went into The

---

[26] https://www.amazon.co.uk/Critique-Reason-Penguin-Modern-Classics/dp/0140447474/ref=asc_df_0140447474/?tag=googshopuk-21&linkCode=df0&hvadid=310805555931&hvpos=&hvnetw=g&hvrand=296978127982303875&hvpone=&hvptwo=&hvqmt=&hvdev=c&hvdvcmdl=&hvlocint=&hvlocphy=20339&hvtargid=pla-433032560534&psc=1&th=1&psc=1

[27] https://thegreatthinkers.org/kant/introduction/#:~:text=His%20moral%20philosophy%20is%20a,can%20have%20no%20moral%20worth.

[28] https://www.goodreads.com/book/show/27712.The_Neverending_Story

Nothing were then born into the realm of humans to live as lies. The Manipulators control The Nothing. Imagine if they had 2030 plan to destroy all fantasy and magic. Replacing fact with fiction, lies and propaganda to create a new world order that they control. Hmmmm... There's something about that last sentence that bothers me, but I can't quite bring it to mind. It must be nothing.

NOTHING FOR CHRISTMAS

One December many years ago, I was asked by a headteacher to work with a 7 year old boy, let's call him Dexter, who was having difficulty settling down in his class. Working with children at Christmas time is so cool usually, as there is a special kind of magic in the air, but not this time.

When I got to the Dexter's house, there was nothing to suggest that we were days away from Christmas, not a card, a tree nor even a piece of tinsel. The property was sterile I felt like I was in an office, not a home. Strange, I thought maybe they follow a certain religion. I met his mother an accountant and his father an I.T. specialist. The parents requested that I did not mention Father Christmas or anything to do with imagination. Their son needed practical help to fit in at school. Dexter preferred to talk to the adults rather than his peers as they, in his words, were *"quite illogical to attempt any communication with"*. Wow! A 7 year olds analyses his classmates and finds them to be immature. The other kids were now avoiding him, which he was quite comfortable with, so where was the problem?

On this occasion, I was at a loss. Dexter was loved by his parents, his home life was logical and practical. The child's grades were excellent, and the parents had agreed for me to see their son on the basis that I could improve Dexter's interactions at school. However, they felt that the school was at fault for promoting imagination and telling the children lies about Father Christmas, etc. After 15 minutes I was already heading to the door, as the parents told me they were leaving to attend an important meeting. My parting words poured out upon the scorched wasteland of our brief communication; slowly, determined and deliberately I said, "Arthur C. Clarke was one of the most influential and important figures in the 20th century. He said, 'Magic's just science that we don't understand yet.' "Merry Christmas to you all!" The front door opened and I stepped out into the cold dark winters night, saddened by the Family Rule of "life is black and white there is no grey," but their lives were exactly that! Grey.

As I reflect on this family, I knew then, that I could work no magic, but I did plant a seed of full colour, which might propagate at a later date, inside the mind of young Dexter. I also glean a little more from Kant. Ever more I look around this world and see people who are massively overweight, unfit, unwell, and unwilling to take responsibility for their actions; they are imprisoned. Kant believed that without freedom people would not have moral appraisal or moral responsibility, their sense of self-worth would not be possible. Perhaps considering our fellow humans as prisoners within a larger system, may explain their lack of responsibility.

And back in the room!

Talking about nothing for a while, kind of loosens and opens the mind, preparing the observer, the listener and the reader for what is to come.

INFINITE POSSIBILITIES

I was given homework by my tutor to complete a montage, some kind of picture or thing that would show to others who I was. This was a classroom assignment that my colleagues and I had to participate in as part of our foundation in counselling course. I hated homework as a child and to be fair, I probably haven't strayed far from that original belief. When the tutor asked us to present our work to the group, I made a hasty dash to the toilets with pen and paper in hand, no pun intended. The result – see image below.

I Am

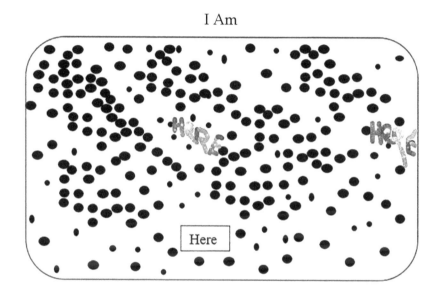

Here

I madly dotted all over the page and wrote "*I am here, for a moment.*" 'This work' I explained was the underpinning of my own personal philosophy: I am constantly popping in and out of existence, beyond the physical to the metaphysical, I am all and I am nothing, I am who you believe me to be, but I am always more, I am infinite possibilities. That was one assignment in the bag only another 30 box ticking exercises to go, I chuckled to myself. However, my devotion to being a life-long learner would drive me to go far and beyond the boundaries of that small classroom in North Tyneside all those years ago.

The reflection above serves as an inroad to this section of the map, it reminds us that life is a journey and yesterday does not equal where you are today. I'm a deaf lad who was born in Wallsend and was raised on a council estate in Walker, Newcastle-upon-Tyne, England, UK. The dialect for my area is called "Geordie," which lends itself to speaking with elongated vowels. A, E, I, O, U, become AA, EE, II, OO, UU. I'm sure you can imagine that I wasn't going to get far in the world if people couldn't understand what I was saying. Education and to be more precise, learning, would be my key to infinite possibilities. My mother always encouraged me with "If you put your mind on it Matthew, then you'll achieve it." How right she was. Although mathematics still continues to create a stir within my amygdala.

When talking of infinite possibilities, it's easy for others to say, "It's alright for you!" So, by beginning with something of your own, sharing a part of your journey to now, helps their mind to create the bridge, where we, you and I connect. Wye aye! Am a deef lad from Waalka and am dee in champion, ye knaa! Translates to: Yes, I'm a deaf chap from Walker and I'm doing fine.

Think choices, futures, and dreams to come true. This is the message of infinite possibilities, where we are limited only by our covert Family Rules. Please keep illness in mind if you are delivering my work to an audience. Many people over the years sneak into a training or a presentation with the hope that they will receive spontaneous remission, if you do well in delivering each step of the map, you may end up as surprised as they were.

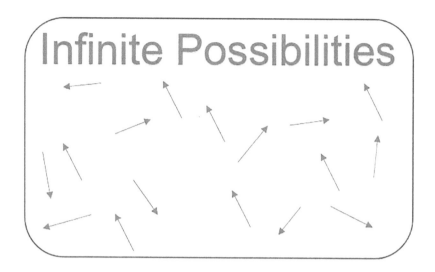

IDENTITY OR *I AM*

Beginning in the centre of the page draw a small stick person and underneath write *"I AM,"* from here we build outwards. Your identity is the who of you in a particular time and place. There are parts of you that appear timeless to others, this is when you bump into someone you haven't seen for 20 years and they say, *"You haven't changed a bit!"* If only they knew the road that you have travelled, the ups and the downs. Too many changes to mention, to even begin contemplating, so you smile and say, "Neither have you!"

If we consider the observer's position then, perhaps we have remained timeless within their mind's eye. The forefather of cognitive neuroscience, Donald Hebb, suggested that the consecutive replay of eye movements allow us to recreate visuospatial relations during episodic remembering[29]. In other words when that friend from the past appears, our past appears. The eye pattern and facial expression are remarkably like the original time that you first saw them, so it's conceivable that you quite literally haven't changed at all!

Your identity can begin as a boy or a girl, then bit by bit you develop and grow. You learn to respond to the sight and sound of your parents, caregivers, and other family members. Then your name "I am John" or "I am Mary", you are a son or a daughter. As you grow, your *I am*'s develop, you can become a "Mammy's boy" or a "Daddy's girl," which may be comforting as a child but as we shall see, these childhood identities have a habit of sticking.

If you have siblings then you will be a brother or sister, first born, second born, third born, or the oldest, the middle son/daughter, the last one/the baby. This all seems straight forward but psychologically it definitely is not. There's a lot of agreement in academia that our personalities are influenced by our birth order. The Austrian psychiatrist, Alfred Adler, "was the first to develop a comprehensive theory of personality, psychological disorders and psychotherapy, which represented an alternative to the views of Freud."[30] His theory of individual psychology looked at you as a whole person, which differentiated his approach to the aforementioned Austrian psychoanalyst. Let's look at how he saw the connection between birth and personality.

---

[29] Johansson R, Nyström M, Dewhurst R, Johansson M. 2022 Eye-movement replay supports episodic remembering. Proc. R. Soc. B 289: 20220964. https://doi.org/10.1098/rspb.2022.0964

[30] Adler A. In: Problems of Neurosis: A Book of Case Histories. Mairet P, editor. New York, NY: Harper & Row, Publishers, Incorporated; 1964.

ADLER'S BIRTH ORDER BELIEFS

First Born Children

Adler's theory suggests that no child is born into the same family environment, which makes sense, as your parents grow a little older and maybe even wiser by the time child number two arrives, child number three and so on. The first-born, initially, receives lots of attention, this amount of attention diminishes upon the arrival of the second child. At this point Adler proposes that the first-born is *"dethroned,"* which can result in the child being motivated towards positive or negative ways to reconcile the attention deficit. This can lead directly to negative or positive life outcomes, in fact researchers have pointed to the first-born as being increasingly susceptible to both drug use as well as positive education outcomes[31].

I've worked with many cases over the years where the first-born, having been out of diapers/nappies during the day and at night, revert to enuresis (when a child, Five years or older, urinates without conscious bladder control). This can prove to be exacerbating for both parents and first-born. The child genuinely does not go to bed wanting to wake up the next morning soaked in cold urine, it's the subconscious motivational traits of the first-born driving this developmental reversal[32]. If you're a first-born reading this then you'll understand exactly what I'm saying, unless of course your mind chose a different set of responses for you to live by. Instead of feeling insecure you rose to the challenge, being a support mechanism for your

---

[31] Laird TG, Shelton AJ. From an Adlerian Perspective: Birth Order, Dependency, and Bing Drinking on a Historically Black University Campus. The Journal of Individual Psychology. 2006;62(1):18–35.

[32] See Kids Now They Come with a Manual for clearing enuresis https://www.amazon.co.uk/Kids-Now-They-Come-Manual/dp/1502380129

younger sibling/s, after all you're the eldest, you should know better! Being the eldest, having your needs met can allow you to develop more leadership skills, as responsibility is laid on your young shoulders from a very early age. This can also make you the family decision maker or influence your caregiving skills.

Whilst reading researcher Mia Kosmiki's study into Hispanic family male and female relationships[33], I discovered two new words, "machismo" and "marianismo."

Machismo – Cambridge dictionary defines as male behaviour that is strong and forceful, shows very traditional ideas about how men and women should behave. Think male Tango dancer!

Cambridge didn't have a definition for "marianismo" so I've gone with Kosmicki's definition, "a gender role script in Latin America, is the concept that women should be the spiritual family leaders, remain abstinent until marriage, and be submissive to their husbands; it originates from the Catholic Church's image of the Virgin Mary." I think the words paint the picture for you.

Both of these gender descriptions come with their own pros and cons in today's society, which has led many adults into poor mental and physical health. Family Rules do not and cannot simply be expunged from a person because social media says so. Gender roles have helped humanity to reach the 21st century and evolution would appear to move forward out of necessity, not a global totalitarian agenda. Oops! I wandered off again, let's get back to birth order.

---

[33] Kosmiki, Mia. Marianismo Identity, Self-Silencing, Depression and Anxiety in Women from Santa María de Dota, Costa Rica. *Cuadernos de Investigación UNED* [online]. 2017, vol.9, n.2, pp.202-208. ISSN 1659-4266. http://dx.doi.org/10.22458/urj.v9i2.1895.

The second or middle child

The second-born child or the middle child (as it maybe in some families), can grow and develop within an environment, where attention from caregivers is shared with the first born. This, Adler believed, would generally cause the second/ middle child to be more cooperative. The reasoning being that the second-born already had a path to follow, which the older sibling had created. The second-born also has the benefit of being able to learn from the mistakes of their older role model. Adler believed that the second-born was best placed than the other birth orders. They were most likely to attune to everyday life. However, the second child and any other child, except for the last or youngest, could still be dethroned.

The last-born, the youngest or 'the baby'

Adler informs us that the last-born wears the invisible crown and can never be removed from the throne. I am the youngest of my family, so I guess I have an opinion to share. I can understand why Adler believes the baby has no followers and can therefore be antagonistic towards older siblings, but there's also the implied support mechanism in the playground. Growing up there were a few bullies around in my school, bullies who had older brothers and sisters. I remember a particular kid, let's call him Fred, who I would put up with until we reached the second year. At our senior school the $3^{rd}, 4^{th}$ and 5th year were on a different site, so the second year left the bullies with no real time backup. The first couple of weeks in September was a readdressing of balance and fairness, or from another viewpoint it was full of fights! Although I was the baby, my brothers and sister were far too old to have an influence in the playground.

I certainly would agree that I tend to be "antagonistic," not with my peers, but with authority. I am very much a free spirit, which has seen me get into all kinds of scrapes. I wouldn't change this part of me, ever! There's also a whole raft of studies which show that the family environment plays a huge role in how our personality develops. For example, studies into adverse childhood experiences (ACEs) [34] have shown early traumatic events can generate recurrent negative symptoms later in life. These impact behaviour, health, personality and a wide range of other physical and psychological conditions[35].

The princess who lost her crown

Sarah was a typical example of dethroning. Although she did not fit exactly with Adler's theory, I had enough insight to witness how her being dethroned was impacting her life. At 28-years old, Sarah's parents had taken her to every specialist on and off for 20 years, desperately trying to find a solution for their daughter's problem. The "problem" as it was presented to me sounded like Crohn's disease[36]. All of the symptoms were there including rectal bleeding, an urgent need to move bowels, abdominal cramps and pain, sensation of incomplete bowel evacuation, constipation, which can lead to bowel obstruction, chronic fatigue, loss of normal menstrual cycle and regular mouth ulcers. This adult woman looked more like a 15-year-old, owing to her poor physical development.

Sarah's parents were truly sceptical of my work, but they had been referred via a psychologist who knew of my success,

---

[34] Felitti, V. J., Anda, R. F., Nordenberg, D., and Williamson, D. F. (1998a). Adverse childhood experiences and health outcomes in adults: the Ace study. *J. Fam. Consum. Sci.* 90:31.

[35] Finkelhor, D., Shattuck, A., Turner, H., and Hamby, S. (2015). A revised inventory of adverse childhood experiences. *Child Abuse Negl.* 48, 13–21. doi: 10.1016/j. chiabu.2015.07.011

[36] https://www.crohnscolitisfoundation.org/what-is-crohns-disease/symptoms

so what's the worst that could happen? This family had been chasing a physical reason for their eldest daughter's illness, yet here they were ready to talk to me without a prescription in sight.

Sarah entered our digital session, and I asked her what she would like to work with? She took a quick glimpse and an intake of breath. Before she had the chance to reply, I asked if she had any brothers or sisters? Again, repeating the same subconscious process, she took another glimpse and another intake of breath. Sarah was first born and had two younger sisters, Claire, second-born and Helen, the youngest. When talking about Claire, the same micro expressions momentarily flashed across Sarah's face, yet there was no shift in breathing or facial tone when I mentioned Helen.

"Your sister wants you dead!" I remarked casually. Sarah's eyes nearly popped out of her head as I went on to explain that she had been dethroned from an early age. Sarah was able to connect deeply with the feelings that somehow matched my statement.

"Obviously she isn't going to hire a hitman or anything like that," I coaxed, "but, did you ever feel that your sister wanted your life?" I reminded Sarah that the session was totally confidential. Even though, Sarah's family wanted her well, they wouldn't want to know that my line of enquiry would have us looking at the attempted murder of their eldest, by their middle child.

Even Sarah couldn't consciously comprehend what I was saying but she could feel that there was something here, something hidden, yet it was there. "She's in everything I do," Sarah said. "My Facebook posts, my friends, WhatsApp groups, everything! I can't breathe, it's like I'm being choked by her." Sarah voiced her frustration and looked ashamed that she was saying it out loud.

Now, you might be thinking, this revelation may cause a massive tear in the family as I work with Sarah to acknowledge how her sister's life dwarfs her own, but hold on and let's just see what happens.

It transpired that when Sarah was away from home at university her symptoms subsided, but upon returning home at the end of her studies she would relapse. There were many different suggestions given as to what might be causing the intermittent flareups: change of diet, water, air, you name it, but no one had successfully treated Sarah, who was now painfully thin owing to an intolerance of practically everything. Did you know that a synonym of intolerance is narrow-mindedness? Sarah's mind had been deleting, distorting and generalising her entire existence to the point where her mind was so narrow, her life felt claustrophobic.

None of this was ever spoken of out loud, within the family. As far as the parents and siblings were concerned, the sisters were both raised well and were trauma free. However, you do not need to suffer at the hand of a physical or mental abuser in order to suffer trauma. Sarah was 18 months old when her abuser arrived, the tiny bundle of joy that would steal all the attention from mummy and daddy, which had previously belonged to her.

This process took about 20 minutes in total, and I was using Sarah's non-verbal communication and body language to gauge how quickly we could move along. Imagine what might happen if I said that's enough for one session, let's meet up next week. The communication loop is open, the client has half an idea which if left to grow, can be used to blame her parents, and most of all Claire for her miserable existence. Wonderful, I think not, puppy dog! Now that Sarah has new learning, it's time to give her even more.

As a learner I've always been curious about how things work, how can someone maintain their problem day in day out for years? I can't even walk into the next room without forgetting what I went in there for, so how do people manage to remember or perhaps a better question is, how can we learn to unlearn?

MEMORY RECONSOLIDATION –

REMEMBERING TO FORGET

In the 1990s a vast amount of research was undertaken in an attempt to find the "holy grail" of clinical procedures within psychotherapy. In other words, faster, positive change. Research has shown that "sudden gains" were possible[37], however 40 years of randomised control trials and meta-analyses of the results showed mild and incremental improvements at best[38]. The idea was to deliver one size fits all treatment models, in the hope that better client outcomes could be consistently achieved[39]. Yippee! An end to poor mental health and happier lives for all, I hear you think, but sadly the idea failed.

The problem seemed to be, after accounting for the therapist's age, years in practice, gender and the type of therapy, there

---

[37] Hayes, A. M., Laurenceau, J. P., Feldman, G., Strauss, J. L., & Cardaciotto, L. (2007). Change is not always linear: The study of nonlinear and discontinuous patterns of change in psychotherapy. *Clinical Psychology Review, 27*(6), 715–723. https://doi. org/10.1016/j.cpr.2007.01.008

[38] Shedler, J. (2015). Where is the evidence for "evidence-based" therapy? *The Journal of Psychological Therapies in Primary Care, 4*(1), 47–59. https://doi.org/10.1016/j. psc.2018.02.001

[39] Truijens, F., Zühlke-van Hulzen, L., & Vanheule, S. (2019). To manualize, or not to manualize: Is that still the question? A systematic review of empirical evidence for manual superiority in psychological treatment. Journal of Clinical Psychology, 75(3), 329–343. https:// doi.org/10.1002/jclp.22712

was zero correlation. It appeared some therapists are just very good at being therapists[4041]. Imagine that! The mechanistic world, where only matter can impact matter, only appears to work in theory. In practice, however, the 'je ne sais quoi' that effective therapists bring to their client sessions was yet to be identified.

There is no doubt the rapid results from some therapists must have an underlying structure or a process that can be followed. Maybe if the researchers had taken the time to do a Google search, they could have saved an awful lot of time and resources. Richard Bandler and John Grinder had already written their seminal work in NLP and produced *The Structure of Magic I: A Book About Language and Therapy*[42]. The authors had by this time modelled successful therapists Milton Erickson, Fritz Perls and Virginia Satir with remarkable results. Yet, seemingly blind to the therapeutic potentials of what NLP had to offer, memory neuroscientists continued their search for an internal mechanism of change[43]. Clinical psychologist Bruce Wampold wrote an excellent article entitled '*The good, the bad, and the ugly: A 50-year perspective on the outcome problem.*' Wampold notes that the effort toward "understanding change in psychotherapy

[40] Okiishi, J., Lambert, M. J., Nielsen, S. L., & Ogles, B. M. (2003). Waiting for supershrink: An empirical analysis of therapist effects. *Clinical Psychology & Psychotherapy: An International Journal of Theory & Practice, 10*(6), 361–373. https://doi.org/10.1002/ cpp.383

[41] Baldwin, S. A., & Imel, Z. E. (2013). Therapist effects: Findings and methods. In M. J. Lambert (Ed.), *Bergin and Garfield's handbook of psychotherapy and behavior change* (6th ed., pp. 258–297). San Francisco: John Wiley & Sons.

[42] https://www.amazon.co.uk/Structure-Magic-About-Language-Therapy/dp/0831400447

[43] Hofmann, S. G., & Hayes, S. C. (2019). The future of intervention science: Process-based therapy. *Clinical Psychological Science, 7*(1), 37–50. https://doi.org/10.1177/ 2167702618772296

is desperately seeking theory". He then went on to state, "not psychotherapy theory."[44] Wow! Just Wow! What he is saying is that psychotherapy theory needs a better theory to support it and that it probably won't come from inside of psychotherapy!

At the turn of the new millennium neuroscience had indeed managed to detect an internal mechanism by which the brain can review and revise the contents of memory, now known as memory reconsolidation. When we recollect a memory or an experience, the chemicals in our brain associated with the event fire up again. Whilst they are in this malleable state, which can last for a few hours, the memories can be altered. When they are reconsolidated by the brain the client gets to keep the change.

The team for me personally who are leading the way with memory reconsolidation, are Bruce Ecker and his colleagues. They have gone from strength to strength with this approach to re-writing traumatic personal history[45]. It seems the secret to successful therapeutic exchanges takes just 3 steps and revolves around learning to unlearn and then to relearn. The empirically proven process below sets out Ecker's work and it answers why I have been able to create rapid changes within my client sessions. I have always maintained that I am a teacher,

---

[44] Wampold, B. E. (2013). The good, the bad, and the ugly: A 50-year perspective on the outcome problem. *Psychotherapy, 50*(1), 16–24. https://doi.org/10.1037/a0030570

[45] Ecker, B. (2018). Clinical translation of memory reconsolidation research: Therapeutic methodology for transformational change by erasing implicit emotional learnings driving symptom production. *International Journal of Neuropsychotherapy, 6*(1), 1–92. doi: 10.12744/ijnpt.2018.0001-0092

not a therapist, therefore the 3 step process sits comfortably with how we will proceed going forward in this book:

1. Reactivation of the target emotional learning
2. Create a mismatch that brings new insight to the experience.
3. Embellish point 1 and 2 to drive unlearning, nullification, and re-encoding of the destabilized target learning[46].

The beauty of working in this style is that both the client and the therapist engage in exploration of the client's presenting problem, resulting in full erasure of the past traumatic event. From a neurochemical position, the cortisol levels that are induced by step 1 are then flushed with dopamine as the client becomes more curious about their 'problem'. Think of it like concentrated orange juice, as you add water the juice becomes more palatable or acceptable to you. Applying a therapeutic intervention with the above 3 steps makes the troublesome emotional learning more acceptable to you. I'm sure there is lots to add, but for now, let's continue to walk through our map.

BELIEFS AND VALUES

I often explain, your identity as a table with four legs. The table's identity is a table, strong solid, has the ability for the family to sit at and eat from, great for parties, special occasions, etc, but it needs four legs to support it. If you break one of the legs then the table ceases to function as a table, or it

---

[46] Ecker, B. & Vaz, A.(2022). *Memory reconsolidation and the crisis of mechanism in psychotherapy*, New Ideas in Psychology, Volume 66, 2022,100945, ISSN 0732- 118X,https://doi.org/10.1016/j.newidea-psych.2022.100945.

becomes an unstable (uns-table read as not a table anymore), its identity is transformed by the action of changing the beliefs and the value of the table will be transformed also. This is the distinction I'll ask you to keep in mind as we go forward. A Family Rule is a fear based limiting belief that is intrinsically tied to survival. Due to the connection these rules have with our stress response system, it becomes glaringly obvious why they need to be cleared. They impact on a person's health, wealth and happiness.

Thoroughly intertwined with your identity, these rules impact beliefs about your identity, meanings, cause, and boundaries. Have you ever wondered what causes you to do something? Why you behave the way you do? Where do you place your personal boundaries, or do you even have any? For now, just think of beliefs as the boundary or the threshold of where you will currently go, what you will currently do, when, how, why you will currently do it and who you are currently being that allows or prevents you from doing it. An invisible parent, forever checking to keep you safe by scaring the heck out of you if you dare to cross the beliefs threshold.

Why can't I sort my Family Rules on my own?

This question is always going to pop up and the number one reason you can't do this work on your own is because the source of your problem is outside of your conscious awareness. As I mentioned at the beginning of this book, when asking clients about their presenting problem they go blank when we get close to the Family Rule. This impasse is the tricky area that we can't get around as it's usually associated with fear, which neuroscience tells us closes down the smart brain. Therefore, if you don't do blank and your thoughts don't go foggy, you will almost certainly come up with something that has nothing to do with your presenting problem – a logical fallacy or red herring! Some people spend years in therapy trying to find the logical reason for their problems. We will discover they are in the mindset of being "uncomfortable not knowing"; this is an unnatural place to be.

The reasoning being that your misleading thoughts are logical (of course) "If I'm feeling (insert feeling) then it (insert modal operator of necessity) be (insert person or external influence) who does this to me. Then freeze the whole process with a nominalisation. Let's call this a "Negative Reasoning Loop".

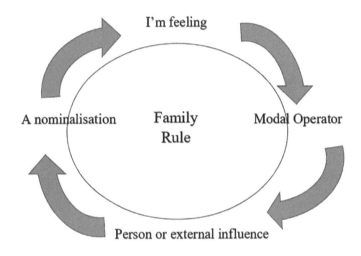

(Take a look at 'Beliefs' by Robert Dilts for a deeper dive[47]).

Personally, I've always set my therapeutic work to align with Milton Erickson, he explained all we ever need to know about therapy and the problems it can create. He believed that the client's problem was like a hot pan, floating between the therapist and the client. The therapist takes hold of the handle, but it leaves the client nothing to hold on to. The client then

[47] https://www.wob.com/en-gb/books/robert-b-dilts/beliefs/9781555520298?gclid=Cj0KCQjwxveXBhDDARIsA-I0Q0x1iwwPJe9u-FOpVUY_Cj8vPnN7GKbCdZuXZ7QkIRK-3gN-5h2e53lOwaAkkTEALw_wcB#GOR004930506

leaves the therapist with a new label, with which to define their problem, but they still have their problem. Therefore, we should aim to do as little as necessary in order to get the best outcome for our client. This is also the underpinning for the MindReset app[48] it aims to create below conscious interventions outside of conscious awareness. Spooky, but cool. I think Erickson would approve.

"We dance round in a ring and suppose,
but the Secret sits in the middle and knows"
Robert Frost

FEAR - FALSE EVIDENCE APPEARING REAL

When we view 'FEAR' as an acronym it gives us a greater possibility to do something about it. We know that the brain can't tell the difference between what is real or imagined. In fact, research confirms that imagination is a neurological reality that can impact our brains and bodies in ways that matter for our wellbeing[49].

A google search will inform you that there are different types of fear. Karl Albrecht Ph.D., in his Psychology Today article[50], points to us having 5 fears:

> **Extinction** — the fear of annihilation, of ceasing to exist. This is a more fundamental way to express it than just

---

[48] https://mindreset.app/
[49] Marianne Cumella Reddan, Tor Dessart Wager, Daniela Schiller. **Attenuating Neural Threat Expression with Imagination**. *Neuron*, 2018; 100 (4): 994 DOI: 10.1016/j.neuron.2018.10.047
[50] https://www.psychologytoday.com/us/blog/brain-snacks/201203/the-only-5-fears-we-all-share

"fear of death." The idea of *no longer being* arouses a *primary existential anxiety* in all normal humans. Consider that panicky feeling you get when you look over the edge of a high building.

Mutilation — the fear of losing any part of our precious bodily structure; the thought of having our body's boundaries invaded, or of losing the integrity of any organ, body part, or natural function. Anxiety about animals, such as bugs, spiders, snakes, and other creepy things arises from fear of mutilation.

Loss of Autonomy — the fear of being immobilized, paralyzed, restricted, enveloped, overwhelmed, entrapped, imprisoned, smothered, or otherwise controlled by circumstances beyond our control. In physical form, it's commonly known as claustrophobia, but it also extends to our social interactions and relationships.

Separation — the fear of abandonment, rejection, and loss of connectedness; of *becoming a non-person* — not wanted, respected, or valued by anyone else. The "silent treatment," when imposed by a group, can have a devastating effect on its target.

Ego-death — the fear of humiliation, shame, or any other mechanism of profound self-disapproval that threatens the *loss of integrity of the self*; the fear of the shattering or disintegration of one's constructed sense of lovability, capability, and worthiness.

I can find a rational argument for each of those five fears being irrational, each of them also require prior learning, so if they were learned they can be unlearned. Therefore, they don't count in our list of fears, they must go beyond the learnt fear, we need something that is inherent for each of us.

In her book *"Do It Scared: Finding the Courage to Face Your Fears, Overcome Obstacles, and Create a Life You Love[51]"* New York Times Best Selling author, Ruth Soukup informs us that we have seven different Fear Archetypes. After completing her study with 4,000 participants, Soukup suggests the fear archetypes include: the Procrastinator, the Rule Follower, the People Pleaser, the Outcast, the Self-Doubter, the Excuse Maker, and the Pessimist. Now, I don't know about you, but I can already think of two or three of these that I fall foul of, but I wouldn't say they were huge fears.

The Procrastinator

The Procrastinator kills time doing all the menial tasks instead of getting on with the job in hand. Take this book for instance, it's only taken me ten years to write, or should I say nine years and eleven months to think about writing it! Getting started is the hardest part, but if you will just jump in and begin, it's like walking into the ocean on a hot summer's day, your first step informs your entire body to STOP! The water is freezing, but if you walk in up to your neck as quickly as possible, or even jump straight in at the deep end, you soon find that everything is just fine.

---

[51] https://www.amazon.com/Do-Scared-Finding-Overcome-Adversity ebook/dp/B07DT3PQNG/ref=as_li_ss_tl?keywords=Do+It+S-cared:+Finding+the+Courage+to+Face+Your+Fears,+Over-come+Obstacles,+and+Create+a+Life+You+Love&qid=1563994291 &s=gateway&sr=8-1-fkmr0&linkCode=sl1&tag=shinetext-20&link-Id=489a98c93008c455e793dbff717a536b&language=en_US

The Rule Follower

I've just given a presentation on this very subject to the World
Council for Health Mind Health Committee, take a look[52]. The
subject title is *"The Subconscious Rule Structure of Compliance."*
Yes, there are people who love to be told what to do, they don't
want to engage their pre-frontal lobe, they just want to know
the right thing to do! I can feel the hairs on the back of my
neck standing up as I think about them. History will show and
you will find out by the end of this book, that fear is a mighty
weapon for getting people to comply. Therefore, if you are a
"Rule Follower" you have a Family Rule running or you have
learned to fear at some point, in either case you can unlearn
it and be free. Without freedom from fear this particular
archetype will live life like an automaton within a mechanistic
world. Imagine that...

The People Pleaser

When surveyed, 40% of the study said they don't practice self-
care as much as they'd like because they prioritize the needs
of others before their own. The *"People Pleaser"* has a fear
running and as you will discover it is tied to a Family Rule.
It's really about how you learnt not to be selfish. The imprint
of the original learning leaves the person without boundaries
as their caregiver assumes that role. Once this Family Rule is
updated it's beautiful to watch the person grow, the energy
that they were haemorrhaging everywhere owing to their
lack of boundaries, is now encapsulated in one place, YOU!
I always update this Family Rule with a cautionary note: the
only people that will be upset with you when you assert your
boundaries are those who were taking advantage of you. Just
a thought...

---

[52] https://www.youtube.com/watch?v=fl0sZE8S0i4

The Outcast

For me, this archetype is tragic and undoubtedly has a Family Rule running, which we will aim to uncover later. Feeling that they are not worthy drives this person to reject love, intimacy, and connection with others before they even get started. They fear being hurt, so they hurt first. They are allergic to commitment! The saddest thing about this archetype is they usually have a very big heart and are desperate to show this, although their attempts to do so backfire as a relationship means pain! If we think in mathematical terms, each human being is a 10 out of 10, you are the only one of you that there is. The problem is you adjust the score, an Outcast will adjust down to a 1 or a 2 out of 10. When a potential partner comes along, let's give them an 8 out of 10, the maths doesn't add up. The Outcast gets with the 8 knowing that they themselves are not good enough for the relationship and can't accept compliments or any information to the contrary. Accepting that they can be loved and loveable would mean that they could be an 8 or more! They would then have to surrender to love, which is a huge step for this archetype, a step that too many are unwilling/unable to take.

The Self-Doubter

This archetype is dominated by the fear of not being good enough. Their identity is the core destabilising element, and you can bet that there is a Family Rule sitting at the heart of the problem. They feel like frauds, working longer and harder to prove to the world and themselves that they are worthy, but even when they get feedback that they are an A grade, they think that the assessment must be incorrect, obviously! If we apply the maths filter again, the Self-Doubter definitely believes that they are a 1 or 2 out of 10. In a relationship Joe

Jackson said it best in his 1979 hit "Is She Really Going Out with Him":

[Verse 1]

Pretty women out walking with gorillas down my street
From my window, I'm staring while my coffee goes cold
Look over there (Where?)
There, there's a lady that I used to know
She's married now or engaged or something, so I'm told

[Chorus]
Is she really going out with him?
Is she really gonna take him home tonight?
Is she really going out with him?
'Cause if my eyes don't deceive me
There's something going wrong around here

[Verse 2]
Tonight's the night when I go to all the parties down my street
I wash my hair and I kid myself I look real smooth
Look over there (Where?)
There, here comes Jeanie with her new boyfriend
They say that looks don't count for much
If so, there goes your proof

[Bridge]
But if looks could kill
There's a man there who's marked down as dead
'Cause I've had my fill
Listen, you, take your hands from her head
I get so mean around this scene
Hey, hey, hey

The song is about a man who is people watching from his apartment window. He is observing Self-Doubters yet as the song progresses, we see that the man is a Self-Doubter who is projecting his own fears onto others and judging them. As the song continues, he gets very angry with the reality of the situation. Why not have a listen?[53]

The Excuse Maker

This archetype avoids situations where they have to take responsibility, they don't want to be held accountable for anything or anyone, not even themselves. This way they can be let off the hook for being overweight, unfit, regularly drinking or eating to excess, running up debts, never beginning their life. "But it's not my fault!" is their default setting as they externalise the blame to the world that owes them. Choosing to allow others to decide on your behalf can work out well, when you are four, but not when you are 40!! There are of course Family Rules at play here, which can be found within the thoughts and wisdom of Immanuel Kant.

Kant's understanding of moral philosophy is a philosophy of freedom. Without human freedom, thought Kant, moral appraisal and moral responsibility would be impossible.[54]I don't know about you, but there seems to be an awful lot of Excuse Makers around these days. When we consider Kant's thoughts in our modern world, we have higher job vacancies since records began in the UK than we have unemployed

---

[53] https://genius.com/Joe-jackson-is-she-really-going-out-with-him-lyrics

[54] https://thegreatthinkers.org/kant/introduction/#:~:text=His%20 moral%20philosophy%20is%20a,can%20have%20no%20moral%20worth.

people[55]. Could it be that the Excuse Maker archetype points to a fundamental problem with the current system that humanity lives in? Why work 38 hours per week when you can make similar money on benefits? Could this archetype be pointing to slavery in the 21st Century? Both parents working full time to afford a rented two bedroomed house and still need access to a food bank to make ends meet, interesting times indeed!

Green Hair Don't Care!

J was the 39 year old female Excuse Maker, recommended to me by a director of human resources (HR) who felt that J could benefit from a development session. When J walked into my office her attitude stepped inside first followed by an anachronistic body. 'Anachronistic' means belonging to an earlier period of time. J was separated from her current chronological age, by at least 25 years. Although our physiological, biological, neurological, psychological, and behavioural responses are always in the present, the *now*, the mind is made of infinite possibilities. We are stardust, sub-atomically popping in and out of the quantum field. Therefore, if there is a glitch in our own time, we can end up with a life that resembles that of the narcissistic weatherman, Phil Connors, played by Bill Murray in the 1993 movie Groundhog Day[56]. In the movie Phil gets trapped in a time loop and wakes up each day with the same day ahead of him, he attempts many ways to escape until eventually he decides to develop and use his time purposefully. Imagine that...

---

[55] https://www.securitywatchdog.org.uk/latest-news/uk-job-va-cancies-higher-than-number-of-unemployed-for-first-time-in-50-years#:~:text=Get%20in%20Touch-,UK%20job%20vacancies%20higher%20than%20number%20of%20unemployed%20for%20first,and%20March%20of%20this%20year.

[56] https://www.imdb.com/title/tt0107048/ Groundhog Day

I don't think J was expecting the kind of approach I use but she had turned up for her appointment and she was going to get an experience that she wouldn't forget. We exchanged the usual pleasantries then I asked how I could help her. J whined on for 15 minutes about how unfair life was to her, her mother, her father, her sister, her teachers, her bosses (she'd had a few) her ex-partners (she'd had a few of those too) on and on blah, blah, blah, she droned. I yawned a big yawn and stretched. Enough, I'm bored now, I thought to myself. Then I thought why keep the thought to yourself Mr Hudson, sharing is caring. In a blink the words were released into the atmosphere between J and I.

"Enough... I'm bored now, aren't you?" I asked in a sleepy, tired, worn-out tone. Slap! The metaphoric custard pie landed and splattered all over J's face. (I will mention at this point that I have mastered this technique, so please be assured that it was done professionally by a master of custard pie throwers). J was visibly rocked by the interruption and before she could respond I asked curiously "How old are you?" J still reeling from the force of the pie, cautiously replied "39."

"Between 3 and 9? I had you down for at least 13, with your green hair and Doc Marten's boots!"

"I am 39" J resolutely affirmed. "39" I said in disbelief. "A 39 year old woman doesn't need help, standing on her own 2 feet, sorting out her finances, getting into a healthy relationship and taking responsibility for her life, does she?" Again J emphasised "I am 39, and nearly 40." This time she was less angry and more assertive. "Nearly 4.... Oooo..!... With green hair and she doesn't care," I mused out loud to myself, as if asking for divine intervention. Often, when I speak from the detached third person position it gives the client space to think, because I have left the room, so to speak.

Noticing the time was nearly up on our session I began to chat politely and pleasantly again, without challenging J, and she left with an indelible puzzled look across her face. I never saw J again, but, about a year later, I did happen to bump into the HR director who had referred her to me. "The crazy thing is" she said, "Jennifer has transformed since her time with you, but she would never admit it". The adolescent J was no more, and the woman Jennifer had claimed her place. If you check out the earlier paragraph, you can see the three steps for rapid therapeutic and long-lasting change were woven into our session. If you can't, then I'm just a cheeky so and so, who has a brass neck and balls of steel, either way the client got the shift she needed.

The Pessimist

This archetype, Soukup states, struggles with the fear of adversity and hardship. This is owing to a past trauma or adverse experience, similar to 39-year-old J who had become stuck. Instead of looking at these events as delays, they see them as denials, which closes the door on their creativity and leads them on a negative loop of self-fulfilling prophecies. The Family Rule in place here is usually born out of over cautious parenting where difference is the thing to fear most. Seeing adversity as a lesson for you to learn from is a really wholesome way for you to examine what has occurred, but the Family Rule will have to be updated before real change can happen, spontaneously.

There are only two Fears

In "*The Saboteur Within*[57]" I highlighted ten fears, eight of which are learnt. Fear of success, failure, rejection, not being liked, loss,

[57] https://www.amazon.com/Saboteur-Within-Definitive-Overcoming-Sabotage/dp/1466336331

helplessness, separation, vulnerability. I give a client example showing how I worked with them to free them from their fear. The other two fears we share with the animal kingdom; these are fear of loud noises and fear of falling backwards. Upon closer inspection the latter two fears appear to be within the bounds of "normal", everything else resides within the mind. That doesn't mean it isn't genuine, it just means that it truly is False Evidence Appearing Real. My next book will go further into fear and its impact on us, so let's leave fear for another day. Back to the next logical step on our map.

Chaos and Confusion

Chaos and confusion sit at the doorway to enlightenment. Yet, many people stand on the threshold of chaos, in a state of confusion. The truth is you cannot be confused over something you know nothing about. Imagine giving a caterpillar flying lessons, the caterpillar is going to be very resistant as he or she has no conscious clue of the amazing transformation they are heading to. That's how I would like you to embrace this part of the map, realise that you will learn, you will grow and you will thrive, thanks to whatever event has thrown you into this area of your mind. This is the challenge that we must all face repeatedly, until we eventually depart this mortal realm to the next stage of our journey. Care for some flying lessons?

When I deliver this part of The Map to an audience, I stand straddled with one foot in fear and the other in chaos and confusion. This is usually where many of us get stuck and begin self-development, devouring books on personal growth, attending trainings or getting one to one coaching/therapy. We, like Neo in the 1999 classic movie "The Matrix" have an itch inside our mind. "The Matrix is the world that has been pulled over your eyes to blind you from the truth…" We cannot be told what the matrix is, we must see it for ourselves."

Morpheus explains to Neo. The "blue pill," Morpheus clarifies, has an amnesic effect, allowing you to fall back to sleep and forget that you ever had this conversation. You've no doubt witnessed this when you've been at a couple's house, after a few drinks they start arguing and it can turn venomous, so you find an excuse to leave. The next day you mention it to your friend, and he/she looks at you like you're the crazy person, they have zero recollection of the night before (Family Rule Alert)! The 'blue pill' serves to maintain the status quo, it allows for no upgrades, just a life of rinse and repeat, which can lead the light in many poor souls to diminish. The 'Red Pill' on the other hand allows you to know the truth, you were born a slave, born into a mental prison that you cannot smell, taste, see, or touch. The red pill is your trip to wonderland to see the real world. My friend if you have read this far, we both know that we are going further down the rabbit hole.

The Natural Entropy of Identity

Sir Isaac Newton's Second Law of Thermodynamics informs us that entropy is the measure of a system's thermal energy per unit temperature that is available for doing useful work[58]. Entropy is formed from the Greek prefix en – meaning "within" and trop- meaning "change." Entropy therefore means "change within a closed system". "Come on, Matt," I hear you say, "what on earth has this got to do with Family Rules and human development?" Humour me just a little longer and hopefully you shall see what I see.

Is what we call a butterfly, the entropy of the caterpillar? Virginia Satir tells us that a closed family system stagnates and diminishes self-esteem, where as a person thrives in an open

---

[58] Drake, Gordon W.F.. "entropy". *Encyclopedia Britannica*, 2 Jun. 2021, https://www.britannica.com/science/entropy-physics. Accessed 21 August 2022.

system[59]. Could it be possible that the majority of humanity in 2022 is nearing entropy, owing to the closed system that is being forced upon us by the global elite, for the greater good? Who's greater good is becoming increasingly apparent at this moment in time.

In his book *"The Psychology of Totalitarianism"*[60], psychology professor Mattias Desmet points to *"Mass Formation"* *"as a kind of group hypnosis that destroys individual's ethical self-awareness and robs them of their ability to think critically."* Desmet points to most of the world population being trapped in social isolation. In the workplace a large amount of absenteeism is due to poor mental health, *"an unprecedented proliferation in the use of psychotropic drugs; a burnout pandemic that paralyzes entire companies and government institutions."* We are all heading for a tipping point, moving naturally toward the entropy of the old system to the reorganisation of a new equilibrium. Maybe check out the Laboratory of Living Matter at Yale University, where scientists are taking a closer look at the energetic expense of biological processes and the associated entropy[61].

Let's wander back from the brink for a little while longer and explore what entropy means to you and me on a smaller scale. We all function within 'systems', the human body for example is psychological, physiological, neurological, etc, several systems that work together in order that we can live. Each of

---

[59] https://www.amazon.com/New-Peoplemaking-Virginia-Satir/dp/0831400706

[60] https://www.amazon.com/Psychology-Totalitarianism-Mattias-Desmet/dp/1645021726/ref=sr_1_1?crid=1HLNIF18LAMCP&keywords=the+psychology+of+totalitarianism+by+mattias+desmet&qid=1661096901&s=books&sprefix=Mattias+Des%2Cstripbooks-intl-ship%2C3484&sr=1-1

[61] https://www.yalescientific.org/2021/04/from-cells-to-thermodynamics-measuring-the-entropy-production-of-living-matter/

these systems looked at separately do not show you or me, because we are the sum of all those systems. For example: if we were to dissect John, one piece at a time and label each part, eventually we would have a bag of parts but no John. John, the owner of the vehicle will cease, he will become the deceased. The physical body is a closed system, yet it still requires an open system to maintain homeostasis or to be more specific allostasis. Homeostasis is the state of our physical internal self, whilst allostasis is the process that our body undertakes to maintain homeostasis.

If we consider for a moment informational entropy, then the psychological impact of information can have a huge impact on our ability to cope or maintain normal life, this impact can be measured as the allostatic load. Allostatic load refers to the cumulative burden of chronic stress and life events. It involves the interaction of different physiological systems at varying degrees of activity. When environmental challenges exceed the individuals ability to cope, then allostatic overload ensues[62].

Information theory, a subfield of mathematics developed by Claude Shannon[63] tells us information must be inversely proportional to probability, meaning the less likely the probability of an event the greater the information. This allows us to view what happens as we leave our current identity and arrive in our new one. Imagine you are in a relationship and your partner comes home every evening at 6.00pm. This information has a high probability, so it costs you very little energy. You don't have to think about it because you know what happens in your home, five nights per week. Today is Tuesday, it's 6.10pm and your partner isn't home, yet. The probability

---

[62] Guidi J, Lucente M, Sonino N, Fava GA. Allostatic Load and Its Impact on Health: A Systematic Review. Psychother Psychosom. 2021;90(1):11-27. doi: 10.1159/000510696. Epub 2020 Aug 14. PMID: 32799204.

[63] https://en.wikipedia.org/wiki/Claude_Shannon

of this happening is very low, so what is happening regarding the amount of information now beginning to run through your mind, it's increasing, right? You start to fill the minutes with stories, you literally flood the void inside your mind with information and the longer you know nothing the greater the information flow. If we were to measure your allostatic load at this point, it would be glaringly obvious that information or rather uncertainty of information is impacting your entire system. When your partner eventually arrives home and you discover that his/her mobile phone battery had died and they had been chatting with someone, missed the first bus and had to catch the next one, your system begins to ease again. Professor Mark Johnson, of Leeds Beckett University, and I are interested in those people who do not exit this informational loop. People who never arrive in the comfort of not knowing and are left in the uncomfortable not knowing state. This, we concur, may be at the heart of all psychophysiological disease[64]. There is one certainty that we do know – uncertainty over long periods of time can be corrosive to the mind and body. Those whose lives are stuck in pause are burning up energy. Vedral Vlatko, Professor of Quantum Information at Oxford and Professor of Physics at University of Singapore, argues in his book "Decoding Reality" that

> *"Life paradoxically ends not when it underdoses on fuel, but, more fundamentally, when it overdoses on 'information' (i.e., when it reaches a saturation point and can no longer process any further information)"*

The bigger question we should all be looking at, according to Vlatko, is "Is it fatal?" Maybe we would all do well to reduce the amount of information we allow into our personal world,

---

[64] https://www.frontiersin.org/articles/10.3389/fpsyg.2021.716535/full

by switching off the digital web that appears to be clouding our minds with more and more useless information and stepping outside, without our phones…a scary or revolutionary thought!

Information ages you

In 2019 I watched a documentary called "Tell me who I am"[65] about the lives of twin brothers Marcus and Alex Lewis. Alex lost his memory at age 18 and relied on his brother to fill in the blanks for him. All was good until the death of their mother, when Marcus revealed that they were sexually abused as children, by their mother's friends and acquaintances. What struck me about the brothers was, although twins, Marcus, who retained all of the graphic memories of their past, looked visibly older than his brother Alex. There are of course studies to show how chronic stress increases inflammation, which accelerates the formation of wrinkles. High amounts of the stress hormone cortisol breaks down the skin's collagen and elastin[66]. We know that trauma ages us, but to see it there on the faces of these twins was alarming!

COMFORTABLE NOT KNOWING

At last, we've reached the end of The Map, free to explore infinite possibilities once more. The "comfortable not knowing" state of mind I likened to the rest of the animal kingdom, with their ability to be fully present in the here and now, without the need of worrying about yesterday or tomorrow.

---

[65] https://www.imdb.com/title/tt10915286/
[66] Lee CM, Watson REB, Kleyn CE. The impact of perceived stress on skin ageing. J Eur Acad Dermatol Venereol. 2020 Jan;34(1):54-58. doi: 10.1111/jdv.15865. Epub 2019 Sep 16. PMID: 31407395.

Life inside the matrix is full of Family Rules that must be obeyed or else. A life overseen by fear and conformity. I like to explain this part of The Map in the following way. Imagine that you have a dispute with someone, you think that you're right and they think that they're right. This costs informational energy that will impact the whole of you. The dispute escalates and they get a solicitor (lawyer for non-UK folk), so you get a solicitor (more information, greater entropy). Eventually you both end up in court with a financial cost of course, but did you ever stop to wonder about the entropy that your system is heading towards? On the day you enter the courtroom, your case is heard by a judge and whatever the judge says is considered to be **Justice**, whether you agree with it or not. Now, let's view this from the position of The Map. All the while you maintain that you are right and they are wrong, you become more and more welded to your map, this blocks the natural flow of information, which leads to greater entropy at a faster rate. Like a shooting star you burn up your life source. If you view the event from outside of your map in a comfortable not knowing state, you receive **Just is** and you are in absolute control of that feeling. Or to put it another way...

"To the mind that is still, the whole universe surrenders."
Lao Tzu

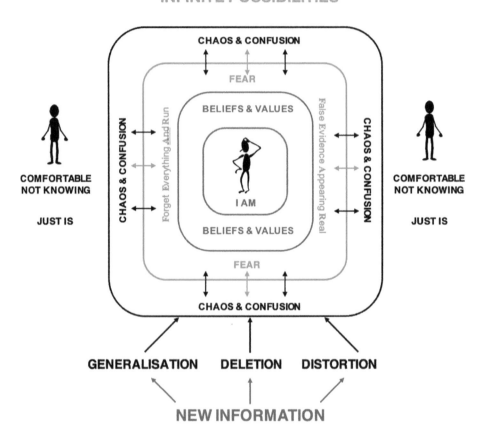

CHAPTER SUMMARY

The Map of the Mind is a way of seeing where you or your client are sticking. Fear will prevent change, so always be aware that there is fear somewhere. Family rules reside between Identity/ Beliefs, Values and Fear. Your client can spend years in Chaos and Confusion, it will impact their physical and mental health. The client may not be ready for the information today but so long as you give them an experience they will shift, on their terms, not yours.

Informational entropy is a potential killer, so unplug as often as you can. Strike up conversations with strangers they may become lifelong friends.

3
WHEN DOES THE GAME BEGIN

*"They are playing a game. They are
playing at not playing a game.
If I show them I see they are, I shall break
the rules and they will punish me.
I must play their game, of not
seeing I see the game"*
R.D Laing

In his book "*Knots,*" Scottish psychiatrist, theoretician, political philosopher, and personal guru Ronald D. Laing invites us to enter the mind of the schizophrenic via pathological poems. You can probably tell from the above extract that there is a deeper structure within the words, the words that tie us in knots, hence the title. If you want a better idea of what it's like to have Family Rules running your life, please invest some time reading Laing's work. "*Knots*" is not for those who do not not want, but for those who do. The knots can be large or small, each comes with its own unique psychological bind to prevent the self from becoming more.

Viewed through a Family Rules lens, the knots are indeed subconscious patterns that create human bondage, binding people together in an invisible, seemingly inescapable game.

As each of us are born we enter the game of life. There are studies that suggest we begin the game as soon as we are conceived, maternal stress during pregnancy impacts the unborn's development[67].

Metabolic functioning – the chemical processes that go on inside of our bodies to maintain homeostasis. Cognitive functions - refers to multiple mental abilities, including learning, thinking, reasoning, remembering, problem solving, decision making, and attention. Emotional Development - how children form and sustain positive relationships, begin to understand who they are, what they are feeling and what to expect when interacting with others[68].

Now, you might be thinking what chance do we have? It's 2022, try and find a pregnant woman who isn't the teeniest bit stressed after the past two years. Luckily for you and I, we remember that we are all knowledge integration devices (KIDs). We are more metaphysical than physical, more nothing than something, popping in and out of the quantum field. We can still have a huge impact on the person, by helping them to go beyond the boundaries of their impoverished mental map.

Setting aside the chemical effects of being held in your mother's womb, vaccines from the medical establishment, and the environment around you, where do Family Rules begin?

[67] Van den Bergh, B., van den Heuvel, M. I., Lahti, M., Braeken, M., de Rooij, S. R., Entringer, S., et al. (2017). Prenatal developmental origins of behavior and mental health: the influence of maternal stress in pregnancy. *Neurosci. Biobehav. Rev.* doi: 10.1016/j.neubiorev.2017.07.003

[68] Zietlow. A, Nonnenmacher. N, Reck.C, Ditzen. B, Müller.M. (2019). Emotional Stress During Pregnancy – Associations with Maternal Anxiety Disorders, Infant Cortisol Reactivity, and Mother-Child Interactions at Pre-school Age *Frontiers in Psychology*. 10(1), [Online]. Available at: https://www.frontiersin.org/articles/10.3389/fpsyg.2019.02179/full [Accessed 22 August 2022].

Perhaps, they begin as we observe the interactions of those around us, our parents, caregivers, siblings, etc. How do they reach each other across the void? From birth our senses are devouring information from the external world. Sight, tastes, smells, sounds are all absorbed, and meanings are created. This conscious and nonconscious learning process continues for the rest of our lives if we are able to remain open to it. There are, however, certain things that remain fixed within the mind as EMIs and whilst protecting us from harm, they may also prevent us from developing.

EMOTIONAL MEMORY IMAGES (EMIS) ARE BARRIERS TO LEARNING

EMIs[69] are mental markers that are created when our system receives negative or positive emotional information. Whenever something similar to the original event/experience occurs, our system replays the original survival response. EMIs are hard wired, rapid responses, that require no conscious input. In the blink of an eye, they will activate the same stress response that was appropriate at the time when we were younger. However, now you are 35, can you see where the problems can occur if you are still running an old operating system?

These "barriers to learning" sit inside our minds eye between us and the outside world, filtering information via our mental map. Do you know why you love or hate cabbage? It's because when you were young, you observed one of your caregivers enjoying or rejecting it. Perhaps, your parents had an argument while you were eating and now you have an allergy to the food you were eating at that time. These mental images have a

---

[69] Hudson & Johnson 2021 https://www.frontiersin.org/articles/10.3389/fpsyg.2021.716535/full

large part to play in whether we just survive or thrive. When researching for information around how the brain might process these emotional images, I determined two key parts of the puzzle: the amygdala and the hippocampus.

The main emotional processing part of the brain is called the amygdala, it combines with the function of the hippocampus to give us declarative and episodic memories. These two brain regions react to the real or perceived environment and drive our motivations. Sometimes, during client work, I would notice that the client's eyes wouldn't move at all, it was like watching someone playing poker. I knew that the information was being processed and that it was activating fear, simultaneously causing the client to follow a subconscious rule structure. But why was there no obvious sign other than there being no sign, which was the obvious sign, if you follow my meaning?

Further brain research informs us that there are there are two amygdalae—one in each cerebral hemisphere. Guess what? One is for visual processing and the other for auditory! Bingo!! The reason for the poker face was because the client processes the rules in sound. Family Rules are not the spoken overt "always brush your teeth before you go to bed." They are the covert internal voice that makes meanings and attaches them to emotions, which remain fixed within the survival mechanism, yet prevent adaptation.

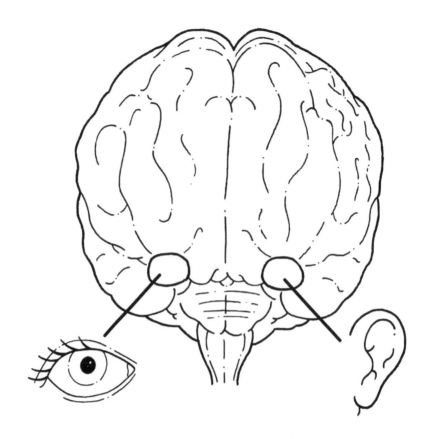

This particular piece of the Family Rules puzzle, though it may seem obvious now, has actually taken a couple of years to reach from the end of the last paragraph to here. I needed to check on a few things in academia before we could progress. The next few paragraphs will bring you up to speed on the mental images side.

There's a lot of research into "mental imagery," especially in and around trauma/ PTSD. In ancient Greece Plato's allegory[70] concerns men imprisoned in a cave, whose only visual stimuli are shadows cast on the wall by objects passing in front of a fire. Those shadows are the only

---

[70] https://faculty.washington.edu/smcohen/320/cave.htm

reality the men experience until they exit the cave and enter the wider world. In other words, Plato is claiming that knowledge gained through the senses is no more than opinion and that real knowledge must be gained through philosophical reasoning. Mental images within the mind can be compared to the shadows projected onto the wall of the cave. These are not reality; they are an illusion, influencing the thoughts and behaviour of those witnessing them. Mental imagery, therefore, sits very close to the root cause of psychophysiological dis-ease.

We know that mental images outside of our conscious awareness can be evidenced by psychophysiological symptoms such as obsessive behaviours, low self-esteem, anxiety, depression, attachment issues, to name but a few (Greenberg 2012[71] Van der Kolk,1994[72] Toomey & Ecker 2007[73]). It's therefore abundantly clear why trauma specialist and researchers have been working to produce a brief, scalable, cost-effective, specific treatment process for reduction of trauma/intrusive thoughts or memories[74]. They

---

[71] Greenberg, L. S. (2012, November). Emotions, the great captains of our lives: Their role in the process of change in psychotherapy. *American Psychologist, 67*(8), 697–707. doi:10.1037/a0029858

[72] van der Kolk, B. (1994). The body keeps the score: Memory and the evolving psychobiology of posttraumatic stress. *Harvard Review of Psychiatry, 1*, 253–265. doi:10.3109/10673229409017088

[73] Toomey, B., & Ecker, B. (2007). Of neurons and knowings: Constructivism, coherence psychology and their neurodynamic substrates. *Journal of Constructivist Psychology, 20*, 201–245. doi:10.1080/10720530701347860

[74] Kessler H, Schmidt AC, James EL, Blackwell SE, von Rauchhaupt M, Harren K, Kehyayan A, Clark IA, Sauvage M, Herpertz S, Axmacher N, Holmes EA. Visuospatial computer game play after memory reminder delivered three days after a traumatic film reduces the number of intrusive memories of the experimental trauma. J Behav Ther Exp Psychiatry. 2020 Jun;67:101454. doi: 10.1016/j.jbtep.2019.01.006. Epub 2019 Jan 25. PMID: 31036259.

are attempting to develop a digital app that can influence the shadows on our own mental wall. For a review of mental imagery check out (Pearson et al. 2015)[75].

Now we are both up to date with mental images, I'm going to point out something very specific about Family Rules. You must be able to comprehend the spoken word for the Family Rule to be created, they cannot be installed pre-verbal. This may sound trivial, but it's a game changer. This means that our next chapter must be dedicated to the birth of meta programs (subconscious filters), so that we can see how we develop our attitude and motivation. Then we will be able to more fully understand where Family Rules fit and why they are so important to our survival.

IN THE BEGINNING WAS THE WORD

I am not an expert on the Bible, but I do remember the phrase "In the beginning was the word". Now, let's set any religious or spiritual beliefs to one side for a moment. In our beginnings, ergo when you and I were born, if we were fortunate, we both had a couple of all encompassing, omnipresent beings who would help us to grow, mentally, physically, and spiritually, yes, our parents. In the beginning their 'word' was everything!

There's a very interesting fact that if we can fit the following eight patterns into our paternal family system then we will be obedient, compliant and let's face it a slave to those who

---

[75] Pearson, J., Naselaris, T., Holmes, E. A., and Kosslyn, S. M. (2015). Mental imagery: functional mechanisms and clinical applications. *Trends Cogn. Sci.* 19, 590–602. doi: 10.1016/j.tics.2015.08.003

rule us. By the way, I'm not suggesting that your parents are totalitarian but let's just take a peek.

1. Would it be fair to suggest that as a child we had limited communication with the outside world?
2. Did our parents encourage us to be proud of our family name and what we stood for?
3. Did we have to tell mum and dad what we were afraid of?
4. Did we always have to be good? This was technically unattainable, so it would leave us with guilt.
5. Could we be punished for attempting to bring in different views or for not following out our parents' wishes without the need for questioning?
6. Were there certain words or phrases that only grown-ups or certain family members were allowed to say? Certain times for things to happen, such as bedtime? Could it extend if parents were pleased or be brought forward if they were displeased?
7. Did the Family Rules come before our individual thoughts or beliefs?
8. Did anyone ever dare mention the black sheep of the family? Was the threat of being cast out of the family ever implied should we do something wrong?

I'm guessing that you may have answered 'YES' to a few of the above questions. The American psychiatrist, Robert Jay Lifton, would suggest you were brainwashed, although he would prefer the term *thought reform*[76]. I'm hoping that you can grasp why a book about family rules needs to have a section on mind control, if you do then this will really help you with your therapeutic work as you attempt to de-hypnotise your

---

[76] Robert Jay Lifton, *Thought Reform and the Psychology of Totalism*, W.W. Norton & Co., Inc., 1963.

clients. If you don't, then obey the voice inside your head and skip this part immediately.

Lifton's work focused on how people who had suffered wartime atrocities or were the perpetrators of them, had the ability to mentally adapt their thoughts. The psychic fragmentation that these people experienced drives the psychophysiological conditions that arise in each of us owing to the stress and fear of the modern society. Some of his most influential books are well worth checking out: *Death in Life: Survivors of Hiroshima* (1968)[77], *Home from the War: Vietnam Veterans – Neither Victims nor Executioners* (1973)[78], and *The Nazi Doctors: Medical Killing and the Psychology of Genocide* (1986)[79]. The latter book helps us to realise that you don't have to be unnaturally cruel, mentally ill, or a sociopath to carry out evil deeds, all you need are the right conditions for this to proliferate. Lifton called this "atrocity-producing situations." In-depth studies of medical professionals were able to rationalise their part in the Holocaust from the commencement of the T-4 Euthanasia Program to the extermination camps. If one was to read *The Nazi Doctors* in parallel with the current medical response to COVID-19 there is a probability of some huge comparisons at play today. Just a thought.

---

[77] https://www.amazon.com/Death-Life-Robert-Jay-Lifton/dp/080784344X

[78] https://www.amazon.com/Home-War-Robert-Jay-Lifton/dp/0671215450/ref=sr_1_1?keywords=Home+-from+the+War%3A+Vietnam+Veterans%E2%80%94Neither+Victims+nor+Executioners&qid=1661238947&s=books&sr=1-1

[79] https://www.amazon.com/Nazi-Doctors-Medical-Psychology-Genocide/dp/0465093396/ref=sr_1_1?crid=2YX8K14X-89WPI&keywords=The+Nazi+Doctors%3A+Medical+Killing+and+the+Psychology+of+Genocide&qid=1661239043&s=-books&sprefix=the+nazi+doctors+medical+killing+and+the+psy-chology+of+genocide+%2Cstripbooks-intl-ship%2C731&sr=1-1

Moving on! Below are the eight processes used to achieve *thought reform*. I just wanted you to see how closely they can align with Family Rules. The following list has been adapted[80]. If you perceive the list through the lens of a paternal system which is supposed to look after us, then it makes a more interesting read:

MILIEU CONTROL

All communication with the outside world is limited, either being strictly filtered or completely cut off. Imagine being locked down in your home, with only the internet telling you one truth, one narrative. Whether it is a monastery or a behind-closed-doors cult, isolation from the ideas, examples, and distractions of the outside world turns the individual's attention to the only remaining form of stimulation, which is the ideology that is being instilled in them. This even works at the intrapersonal level, individuals are discouraged from thinking incorrect thoughts, which may be termed evil, selfish, disinformation, "anti-woke."

MYSTICAL MANIPULATION

A part of the teaching is that the group has a higher purpose than others outside the group. This may be altruistic, such as saving the world or helping people in need. It may also be selfish, for example that group members will be saved when others outside the group will perish.

All things are then attributed and linked to this higher purpose. Coincidences (which may be deliberately engineered)

---

[80] http://changingminds.org/techniques/conversion/lifton_thought_reform.htm

are portrayed as symbolic events. Attention is given to the problems of out-group people and attributed to their not being in the group. Revelations are attributed to spiritual causes. This association of events is used as evidence that the group truly is special and exclusive. "We follow the science!" according to the chief medical officer of the United States of America, Anthony Fauci[81].

CONFESSION

Individuals are encouraged to confess past 'sins' (as defined by the group). This creates a tension between the person's actions and their stated belief that the action is bad, particularly if the statement is made publicly. The consistency principle thus leads the person to fully adopt the belief that the sin is bad and to distance themselves from repeating it. Discussion of inner fears and anxieties, as well as confessing sins is exposing vulnerabilities and requires the person to place trust in the group and hence bond with them. When we bond with others, they become our friends, and we tend to adopt their beliefs more easily. This effect may be exaggerated with intense sessions where deep thoughts and feelings are regularly surfaced. This also has the effect of exhausting people, making them more open to suggestion.

SELF-SANCTIFICATION THROUGH PURITY

Individuals are encouraged to constantly push towards an ultimate and unattainable perfection. This may be rewarded by promotion within the group to higher levels, for example

---

[81] https://www.nationalreview.com/2021/11/anthony-fauci-i-am-the-science/

by giving them a new status name (acolyte, traveller, master, etc.) or by giving them new authority within the group.

The unattainability of the ultimate perfection is used to induce guilt and show the person to be sinful, hence sustain the requirement for confession and obedience to those higher than them in the groups order of perfection. Not being perfect may be seen as deserving of punishment, which may be imposed by the higher members of the group or even by the person themselves, who are taught that such atonement and self-flagellation is a valuable method of reaching higher levels of perfection.

AURA OF SACRED SCIENCE

The beliefs and regulations of the group are framed as perfect, absolute, and non-negotiable. The dogma of the group is presented as scientifically correct or otherwise unquestionable. Rules and processes are therefore to be followed without question, any transgression is a sin and hence requires atonement or other forms of punishment, as does consideration of any alternative viewpoints.

LOADED LANGUAGE

New words and language are created to explain the new and profound meanings that have been discovered. Existing words are also hijacked and given new and different meaning.

This is particularly effective due to the way language affects how we think. The consequence of this being the person who controls the meaning of words also controls how people think. In this way, black-and-white thinking is embedded in the language, such that wrongdoers are framed as terrible and evil, whilst those who do right (as defined by the group) are perfect and marvellous.

The meaning of words are kept hidden from the outside world, giving a sense of exclusivity. The meaning of special words may also be revealed in secret societies, where people elevated within the order are given the power of understanding this new language.

DOCTRINE OVER PERSON

The importance of the group is elevated over the importance of the individual in all ways. For 'the greater good." Along with this comes the importance of the group's ideas and rules over personal beliefs and values. Past experiences, beliefs and values can all thus be cast as being invalid if they conflict with group rules. In fact, this conflict can be used as a reason for confession of sins. Likewise, the beliefs, values, and words of those outside the group are equally invalid.

DISPENSED EXISTENCE

There is a very sharp line between the group and the outside world. Insiders are to be saved and elevated, whilst outsiders are doomed to failure and loss (which may be eternal). An outsider or insider is chosen by the group. Thus, any person within the group may be damned at any time. There are no rights of membership except, perhaps, for the leader.

People who leave the group are singled out as particularly evil, weak, lost or otherwise to be despised or pitied. Rather than being ignored or hidden, they are used as examples of how anyone who leaves will be looked down upon and publicly denigrated. People thus have a constant fear of being cast out, they consequently work hard to be accepted so not to be ejected from the group. Outsiders who try to persuade the person to leave are doubly feared. Dispensation also goes into all aspects of living within the group. All aspects of existence within the group are subject to scrutiny and control. There is no privacy and, ultimately, no free will. Hmm…! That's interesting.

It's worth noting that Lifton was one of the first to organise talking therapies for Vietnam veterans. He lobbied to have PTSD included in the Diagnostic and Statistical Manual of Mental Disorders (DSM). The World Health Organisation back in 2013[82] stated that many people will experience trauma during their lifetime, heaven only knows what the traumatic toll is today.

My reasoning for pointing to Lifton's work in this chapter is hopefully becoming clearer. In my 25 years of practice, I have asked parents to raise their hands if they have ever woken up at 3.00am with a burning desire to screw up their children's lives. To date, no parent has raised their hand. Yet, my clinic was full of adults who blamed their parents!

Lifton tells us that it doesn't require people to be inherently evil for bad things to happen, it just takes the right circumstances. Parents have immense pressure put upon them to raise their children in a certain way. Moral and spiritual values are being eroded and replaced by a financially homogenised, safe existence, where relationships are transactional and dispensable. Family connections, the roots from which we feed, develop, learn and grow are being fragmented. In these

---

[82] WHO (2013). *Guidelines for the management of conditions that are specifically related to stress.* Geneva, Switzerland: World Health Organization.

environments good people may do bad things. A meta-analysis in 2017 revealed that over 1 billion children had suffered trauma having been exposed to violence and victimisation[83]. The results of a national survey in the USA points to two out of three children suffering from adverse childhood experiences (ACEs)[84].

Given what we have discovered so far about Family Rules and how the brain is hard wired to continually repeat the past, it isn't difficult to see how adverse events can happen inside what on the surface seems to be a "normal" family. These traumas whether deliberate or accidental, large or small, are stored inside an EMI, which over time may lead to the child becoming the parent and re-enacting their childhood on their children.

Hopefully, you're able to grasp the hypnotic state that can be induced by these mental images, many of which, just like Family Rules, are stored and activated subconsciously, with little to no conscious awareness. Sometimes bringing these rules to the surface, into the light, can be enough for them to resolve. Stepping into the light brings apprehension, but one must remember that as a 2-year-old we did not fear stepping up. We were born fearless, a Warrior! What if our society is being taught, manipulated, suppressed, and scared into believing that we are *Worriers*!

Perhaps, the modern digital world is adding to the splintering of our humanity, we are first and foremost social creatures,

[83] Hillis, S. D, Mercy, J. A, & Saul, J. R. (2017). The enduring impact of violence against children. psychology. Health & Medicine, 22(4), 393-405.
[84] Finkelhor, D., Turner, H. A., Shattuck, A., & Hamby, S. L. (2015). Prevalence of childhood exposure to violence, crime, and abuse: Results from the national survey of children's exposure to violence. JAMA Pediatrics, 169(8), 746–754.

without "social" we may fast become "creatures." Just existing, trapped like insects, caught in a worldwide web. Maybe I need to take a break here, step away from the computer and converse with Lisa about where this chapter has brought us. As Desmet says in his new book *The Psychology of Totalitarianism*[85] "Digitisation dehumanises a conversation" so make sure that you chat with a real human being today, it's good for your health and theirs.

The *Word*, as this chapter closes, truly is at our beginning. The voice of our parents resonates within and around us. A divine metronome, to which we are attuned, keeping time, setting the pace, from which our own unique signature tune arises. Even though my parents, my brothers and my sister have left this realm, I can still feel their echo deep within.

EXERCISE - A WORD

This is a fun exercise to do with another person.

1. Both of you think of a word that best describes you. Yes, just one word.
2. Communicate to each other using only this word, nothing else.
3. Keep going for as long as it takes for one of you to break the pattern.

The idea is to get onto the other person's map of the world using only your word.

I played this game on a training held by Wilf Proudfoot years ago. It was a sunny day, and I was wearing a vest and shorts,

---

[85] https://www.amazon.com/Psychology-Totalitarianism-Mattias-Desmet/dp/1645021726

so the word I chose was "Hair", I'm a hairy guy. Anyway, I partnered up with a lady whose word was "Poltergeist!" Now I ask you, what sort of chance did I have? About 30 minutes into the game the rest of the group had finished and gone to lunch, I was hungry, but I wasn't going to give up. I sat, leant forward to put my head in my hands and faced the floor. The thought of food got my saliva going. All the while I'm listening to this witch (her description) giving it "Poltergeist! Poltergeist! Poltergeist!" Then, I realised that I was failing to connect with my partner. I needed to get onto the same wavelength as a witch. I built up a mouthful of saliva, raised my torso, then my head, stared her straight in the eye and yelled "Hair!!!" Like a zombie, whilst allowing the saliva to dribble down my face. "You're sick!" she yelled at me. "Lunch!" I grinned back at her.

CHAPTER SUMMARY

We've covered the subconscious influences of Family Rules and how traumatic events can create emotional memory images.

Words can have powerful meanings, which is probably why we learn to spell. Spells have magical connotations. Words and rituals can be used to manipulate us outside of our awareness. Make sure that you maintain human connections not just digital ones.

4
THE STRUCTURE OF COMPLIANCE

> *"If a law is unjust a man is not*
> *only right to disobey it,*
> *he is obligated to do so"*
> Thomas Jefferson

These are wise words from Thomas Jefferson, but what if the family were unaware of what was happening? What then? In the last chapter we looked at the power of the word and how within the family - paternal system - it is possible to manipulate others by applying certain rules. To help us better understand what 'paternal' means I am using the Stanford Encyclopaedia of Philosophy definition. Paternalism - Paternalism is the interference of a state or an individual with another person, against their will, and defended or motivated by a claim that the person interfered with will be better off or protected from harm. The issue of paternalism arises with respect to restrictions by the law such as anti-drug legislation, the compulsory wearing of seatbelts, and in medical contexts by the withholding of relevant information concerning a patient's condition by physicians. At the theoretical level it raises questions of how persons should be treated when they are less than fully rational.[86]

---

[86] https://plato.stanford.edu/entries/paternalism/

About ten years ago a very dear friend of mine, Henk Beljaars, and I chatted for a long while about subconscious motivational drivers. What makes us do the things that we do? In NLP these motivational drivers have been broken down and codified as meta programs – below conscious filters that sift the incoming information from our external environment to fit our mental map of the world. We had a bone to pick, and it took a while chewing it over. We'll get to that before the end of this chapter, first let's look at how meta programs are formed, as it follows on nicely from the word. Just hold the thought of an Englishman and a Dutchman conversing at a bar.

AH! THE FIRST STEP TO COMPLIANCE

I'd like you to imagine you are about 18 months old, wandering about in your safe environment as you were earlier in Chapter 1, no spiders this time! I want you to reach out towards something, something interesting, maybe the flames in the fire, for instance, closer and closer, closer, and closer, then "AH!" thunders the voice of your caregiver. Your amygdala shuts down your curiosity and engages the stress response of freeze. The *freeze* response is the most logical survival decision, your caregiver is present, there is no need to run or fight, so freeze! Their intonation is inflected downwards, and it booms through the air, a wall of sound, a mental leash that commands you to halt! Stop what you are doing! Obey me, now!!!

The amazing thing is, little you understands all the above meanings and more. In a split-second you've learnt the *Away From* Pattern. This will motivate you to avoid situations where problems might occur. As you develop and your parents can see that you understand and comply with "Ah!" the next stage in your development is met with "Ah, Ah!". This means that you may have forgotten what you should or shouldn't do here, so remember. "Ah, Ah!" allows for a slackening of the leash and gives you space to notice that there is a decision to be made.

Assuming that you have passed the previous step with flying colours, you will naturally progress to the final stage "Ah, Ah, Ahhhh!" meaning we both know that you shouldn't be doing that so do this instead. "Ah, Ah, Ahhhh!" means go towards something else. Mastering this final step means you have just passed your first driving test. From here on you are able to manoeuvre away from pain, towards pleasure. Depending on the influences of your parents and family members, you may develop a particular craving for one over the other in certain circumstances. See the diagrams below for more detail.

DIRECTION

AWAY

AWAY FROM (OR FOLLOWER):

These people are avoidance oriented, motivated to move away from problems. They talk about what they don't want, want to avoid, prevent, get rid of, get away from. They'll talk about *excluding* things, people, and situations. Their behaviour may cause the body to shift back as they communicate what they don't want. They spend their time 'fixing things', fighting fires and solving the problem of the moment. They are distracted by every small problem that catches their attention, so they often lose track of targets and priorities. You can motivate them by pointing to what we want to prevent/avoid/exclude, "the problems to be solved," or "the stuff we won't have to worry about."

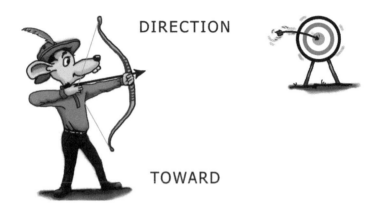

DIRECTION

TOWARD

TOWARD (OR STARTER)

These folks stay focused on their goals, thinks in terms of what is to be achieved, what they're going to get, gain or have. They talk about achieving goals, making gains, reaching targets, what they will do. They'll talk about *including* things, people and situations. Stay focused on priorities, goals, tasks, and what they want to achieve. They may lean forward when communicating this. In their enthusiasm to reach the target they may overlook potential obstacles. They lose their motivation if forced to continually spend their time solving problems. You can motivate them by saying what they will achieve," "this is the goal/target," "you will be able to accomplish," use words like achieve, create, attain, include, have, get, gain.

Now, we have the direction filters built in the next logical step is your **reason** for doing something. Do you like **Options** or a **Process**?

REASON

Options

These individuals need lots of choice, alternatives, are good at creating options and have difficulty following procedures. They may change their mind frequently and resist making decisions. They find it difficult to follow directions and like to challenge the system, bend the rules, find loopholes. They resist following procedures. Motivate them by asking them to "Consider all the possibilities in this project," "you'll have unlimited choices," "let's find a new way to do this," "be as creative as you like" "to keep all your options open you'll have to decide now," "you can do it," "the only way to have a choice later, is to do this now."

Process

Process driven people are excellent at maintaining systems and consistently following step-by-step procedures.
They do "necessary" things and once started on a procedure want to follow it through to completion. Say to them "Consider your obligations to do it the right way," "we always do it this way," "this is the procedure we'll follow, step one is…"

They may have difficulty recognising when a process no longer works. Give them assistance to fix the procedure and they'll follow it faithfully until it needs fixing again.

They don't like options – Freedom is an option!

SOURCE

The next logical step could be how do you know what's right and what's wrong? Where do you **source** your information? Do you just know (internally referenced) or do you rely on sources outside of yourself (externally referenced.)

Internal

These people are motivated by internal standards and beliefs. They will use the first person singular "I", decide about the quality of their work and have difficulty accepting outside opinions or direction. *They treat instructions as information then make their own decision about what needs to be done and when to do it.* They reject feedback unless it matches their internal feelings. As managers, they only give feedback when dissatisfied. You can influence them with statements like "I can't convince you... only you can decide," "It's your decision," "you may want to consider... and once you have considered..." "you'll realise that" "for the information you need to decide just call."

External

These people do not have internal standards, but rely on external standards. They require continuous feedback to know the quality of their work and value the opinion of others. *They take information as instructions and may change their priorities based on casual comment about what is possible.* They frequently refer to what others think, say, or do.

Influence them with "Here is what others are saying/doing," "you'll get good feedback," "this is how you'll know," "everyone agrees the best way is…" "the experts recommend…" "… has improved this."

The patterns we have covered so far are enough to get us to function beyond the level of an amoeba. Once upon a time I would have said that last line with great confidence, but these days science informs us that even the single celled organism has these basic functions.[87]

ACTION LEVEL

Now that we know which direction we want to take, our reasoning behind taking it whether we've just decided it's the right thing to do or the guy on the television told us; we need to decide what level of action we should take.

---

[87] De la Fuente, I.M., Bringas, C., Malaina, I. *et al.* Evidence of conditioned behavior in amoebae. *Nat Commun* **10**, 3690 (2019). https://doi.org/10.1038/s41467-019-11677-w

Proactive

Someone who initiates, likes to make things happen and is always busy "doing." They sound like they are in control of their world. Even when sitting they continuously move and shift their body around.

They are known to act quickly and may jump in without taking a lot of time to consider the situation. Influence them by saying "Let's get this project started," "go for it," "make it happen," "jump on it," "Just do it," "take action," "will do."

Reactive

Reactive people like to analyse and consider the situation, waits for others to initiate action. They talk about considering, studying, analysing, what they could, should do. They are comfortable with long periods of inactivity and can sit in relative stillness for long periods.

Influence them with "Now that you've had time to consider this" "You might, could, would" "It's OK to take all the time you need to make a decision now" "consider" "understand", "wait, think about, analyse."

FOUR PATTERNS OF DIS-EASE

You may have spent time with people who have a predisposition to being low on energy. So much so, that you feel flat as you read these words just thinking about them. Yes, those people! Is it possible that they wake up every day wanting to feel this way? The logical answer is, of course, "No!" Knowing what we've learned so far may help to shine light on the situation for those individuals. What if when they were children onboarding information, like we've just been doing in the examples above, something went wrong? What if they are trapped within a hypnotic informational loop, their life would fast become Groundhog Day! This is where I have met many, many individuals over the years, dehypnotised them and broke the trance that they learned. Unlearning can genuinely take a split-second.

Let's take one out of each of the patterns above and mix them. For example, you've not been feeling very well for the last couple days. You're not eating and have a pain in your tummy. You think to yourself, "It will pass," and just put up with it. This translates into:

Away From	You're avoiding doing anything.
Options	Doing nothing is a choice.
Internal	You make the decision.
Reactive	You are thinking, not doing.

By day four you haven't slept well. The pain is a little worse. You decide to take an aspirin, or maybe there are some leftover antibiotics in the back of the cupboard. You consider having a look on Google to see what your problem might be. This translates into:

Away From	with a dash of **Towards** – You're beginning to move toward help.
Options	Different choices are popping into your head.
Internal	with an external check to see if Google agrees with you.
Reactive	thinking about Googling.

By day five the pain is now agonising, you are double bent in the fetal position. You dial 911 and an ambulance arrives to take you to hospital. You are diagnosed with appendicitis and told that you must undergo emergency surgery now, or you will be dead by teatime.

Towards	The pain has forced you to move toward.
Process	Calling 911 began the process, you are going to have a medical procedure.
External	You are now allowing the hospital to take charge of you.
Proactive	You made the call.

Yes, the example may be a little drastic, but I hope you get the idea. What would happen if you'd had an adverse childhood experience (ACEs) but you weren't consciously aware of it? We've discovered in previous chapters that this is possible. Wouldn't an emotional memory image activate the freeze response each time it was triggered? This could increase your away from, as your smart brain would cloud over whenever you tried to think your way out of the hypnotic loop. Then as you got a little older and develop language, the Family Rules would begin to underpin the narrative, which would in turn become your life script.

MARY'S STORY

Mary had booked for a session with me, after a referral from her doctor. Mary was a few weeks away from her 60th birthday and since she'd tried everywhere else, why not come and see me? I'm reliably informed that the reader (that's you) likes to hear about their symptoms and how long they have suffered. This always causes me a problem because I don't need the client's story to help them. I'm going to explain Mary's session to you as it happened and then fill in the symptoms part afterwards. This way, you can understand more fully how I work. Mary arrived with her husband, who was to act as her translator should she not be able to understand my English. I prefer to think of John (her husband) as emotional support. Our session took place inside the doctor's clinic, so I was behind a desk, which was very unusual for me as Mary seemed so far away. I invited John to sit at my side of the desk, so that he could be my assistant. Yes, it's unusual in anyone else's clinic, but not mine.

I looked at Mary and asked, "How can I help you today?" She took a deep breath, while her eyes simultaneously flicked up to her left. Before she could answer, I turned to John and asked him if he noticed anything happen, just then? A very confused John replied "No." This is a very good answer, at least he's honest enough to say when he sees nothing. I then instructed John to look more closely this time. Looking at Mary I repeated "How can I help you today?" She dutifully reiterated her problem by taking a deep breath, while her eyes simultaneously flicked up to her left. "John?" my voice inviting my new colleague's observations of our client.

"I saw something!"

"Well done! Can you be more specific?" I enquired.

"No," he replied.

"That's okay," I encouraged, "this is your first patient, after all."

I then explained to John that Mary's eyes moved up to the left and she took a deep breath in.

"Yes, yes! That is what she did!" John said triumphantly.

I broke down what John saw, so he knew he wasn't just agreeing with me for the sake of it. When he said he saw something he was correct, but it happened so fast that he could only rely on his gut feelings, which told him something had moved.

Mary sat watching John and I discussing her non-verbal response to my one question. I'll explain this in a moment but first let's finish the session and get Mary sorted.

"Are you ready?" I asked John, he nodded. Looking at Mary for the third time I asked, "How can I help you today?" Before she could answer John said, "She's changed!" I smiled a big cheesy smile. "She has indeed, John."

"Can you elaborate?" I asked.

"She didn't do the breath this time and her eyes are somewhere else"

I congratulated John for being a fantastic student. Then turning to Mary, I asked "Is there anything else that you would like to work with?" A very confused Mary smiled at us and said "No." The session ended and they left.

Now, back to Mary, I prevented her from verbalising her problem. This is a technique that I have spent a lifetime mastering. If you read *The Saboteur Within*, you can see that I use the same technique to clear the boy's stammer. It's a rapid process for interrupting the information loop created by the emotional memory image. Does it work all the time? No. As we learnt earlier some traumas are maintained visually and some auditorily, on this occasion it was an image that needed to be removed. If the client starts to download their problem, the neurochemical state they get themselves in blocks the process, so I get in quick before they can arm up their defence system.

Further to this, Mary is observing her husband and I am observing her. This is only going to maximise her curiosity. Curiosity is connected to dopamine, the neurotransmitter associated with reward (think big bar of chocolate). Before Mary had her "problem" she was comfortable not knowing and curious about life, this state of mind was producing dopamine. When her problem began, her freeze stress response continually flooded her system with cortisol and adrenaline. The fear response our system chooses influences these 2 main stress chemicals[88]. In Mary's case her adrenaline was causing her major problems as her system was trying to outrun the threat inside her mind. This is a natural response to a threat; however, the predator was invisible to Mary and all the consultants she had visited over the past 40 years. Just read that last sentence again…for 40 years this wonderful lady was in bed by 7.30pm at the latest, worn out, shattered and unable to stay awake. If I allow Mary to give me her diagnosis then I will be the professional taking hold of the handle, (Erickson's words reverberate) leaving Mary with nothing to hold onto. If I step onto Mary's mental map, I am up against doctors

---

[88] Kozlowska K, Walker P, McLean L, Carrive P. Fear and the Defense Cascade: Clinical Implications and Management. Harv Rev Psychiatry. 2015 Jul-Aug;23(4):263-87. doi: 10.1097/HRP.0000000000000065. PMID: 26062169; PMCID: PMC4495877.

and consultants, the words of a teacher will not penetrate her clinical understanding of her problem. We don't go there! (I can see my buddy Henk smiling at this). I'm a teacher, I teach you how to unlearn what you have experienced by giving you a better learning experience. It really is that simple.

The following month Mary and John booked a second session. They came to ask the best way to explain her recovery to their family and friends. Sometimes, change can happen too quickly for everyone else, I suggested that they don't look so happy all of the time! Believe it or not it's true.

ADVERSE CHILDHOOD EXPERIENCES (ACEs)

It's apt that we should look at ACEs in a book about Family Rules. Some of the adverse experiences we have as children may be stored auditorily; meaning there is a voice inside your mind that is driving psychophysiological problems for you. Other ACEs may be stored as emotional memory images and as in the case of Mary and thousands of others.

Mary's story resembles a lot of the symptoms people suffer with today, fatigue and lack of energy being highly prevalent. If you run anxiety for 20 years, you can expect to reach fatigue by a similar route, as the years of overworking the adrenal glands takes its toll. What if you a have psychophysiological disorder, (which is difficult to diagnose by the way), but you have no conscious memory of ever having a traumatic experience as a child? You would never consider a trauma treatment because it doesn't make sense, right? But we've learned that our mind can store threat responses subconsciously, outside of our awareness, so who knows.

If you think this sounds difficult to get your head around as an adult, then spare a thought for the children as childhood trauma is very difficult to diagnose[89]. This is especially true if your experience happened when you were a baby before you learned to talk[90]. Preverbal trauma means you wouldn't have been able to express or convey to your parent what had happened or was continuing to happen. If you are fortunate enough to get treatment as a child, it will probably take the form of working with somatic memories or play therapy[91]. When you take into account the range of ACEs that can impact our development it's not surprising that so many of us suffer mental and physical health conditions on a daily basis.

ACEs can be caused by physical, sexual or mental abuse but it can also be owing to loss – which covers death, divorce, even moving home. Emotional or physical neglect can occur easily if your parents themselves are suffering, remember given the right conditions good people can do bad things. When you are growing up witnessing adults with alcohol or drug problems, their mental state can impact yours. The list goes on, I just want you to know that you may have suffered a trauma, which has created an emotional memory image. If you can perceive this as a barrier to learning, then we can transform this caterpillar into a butterfly.

_____

[89] De Young, A. C., Kenardy, J. A., & Cobham, V. E. (2011). Trauma in early childhood: A neglected population. Clinical Child and Family Psychology Review. doi:10.1007/s10567-011-0094-3.

[90] Coates, S.W. (2016). Can Babies Remember Trauma? Symbolic Forms of Representation in Traumatized Infants. *Journal of the American Psychoanalytic Association, 64*, 751 - 776.

[91] Spiel, S., Lombardi.,K & L,. DeRubeis-Byrne. (2019). Treating traumatized children: somatic memories and play therapy. *Journal of Infant, Child, and Adolescent Psychotherapy, 18*(1), 1–12.

THE *ACES* PYRAMID

The below diagram shows the impact of ACEs over a lifetime[92]. Take a few minutes to absorb what this chart is telling us. Years of running stress chemicals is toxic and corrosive to our body, not to mention the stuff we expose ourselves to such as alcohol, sugar, or worse.

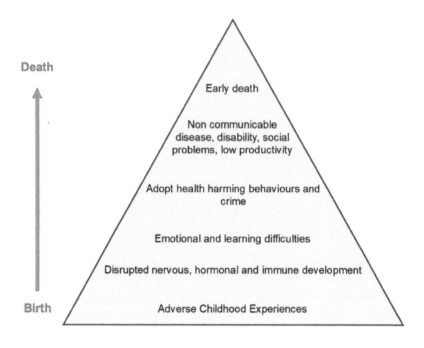

THE MISSING RULE STRUCTURE

As I was saying earlier, Henk and I talked a long while about "Rule Structures" the subconscious instructions that you abide by in certain situations or contexts. I'll give you the list of what is current and then we can look at how Henk and I arrived at our conclusion.

---

[92] https://www.cdc.gov/violenceprevention/aces/about.html

My/My

My rules for me/**My** rules for you

They know what they have to do and will tell you what others should do. They have rules to manage their own behaviour and the same rules for others; they expect others to be like them.

You can influence them by telling them "You know what you have to do, and you know what the others have to do."

My/. (Full stop)

My rules for me/**. (Full stop)**

My rules for me, I don't know about others. Can tell you what they have to do, will tell you they don't know what others need to do.

Influence them with "You know what you have to do, and it isn't important for you what the others do."

My/Your

My rules for me/**Your** rules for you

Can tell you what they should do but they won't presume to tell others what to do.

Influence them with

"You know what you need to do, and you can let the others decide for themselves."

No/My

No rules for me/**My** rules for you

Have no rules for themselves, can tell you what others need to do *because 'someone else'* will have told them.

They can be influenced with "Now that you've been told what to do you can pass the instructions along"

No/My can also use phrases like: "Do as I say not as I do" or "One rule for thee another rule for me."

DID YOU SPOT WHAT'S MISSING?

If you managed to spot the missing pattern well done. The rest of us will continue reading, while you go make a coffee and wait for us to catch up. No/My is a rule structure that sits behind Family Rules, and one might conclude that it falls within ACEs too. The person who has no rules for themselves but is willing to inflict rules on others falls under the guise of a dictator. Mattias Desmet eloquently sums up this pattern in his new book *The Psychology of Totalitarianism.*[93]

> *"The totalitarian leader differs from an idealist in that he shows a radical, fanatical blindness but definitely also because of a remarkable lack of principles and aversion to laws. For example, he typically rules by decree on the basis of temporary rules that can be adjusted at his discretion. The*

---

[93] https://www.amazon.com/Psychology-Totalitarianism-Mattias-Desmet/dp/1645021726

only law he really upholds is that there are no laws!" Mattias Desmet (2022).

The **No/My** tells us how a family system may be dysfunctional. The work of Lidz, we discovered earlier, can tell us (a) if it's just delusional parents *folie à deux*, or (b) the delusional reality is shared by the whole family *folie en famille*. The family members will suffer, stress, anxiety, depression, mental health problems, physical health problems, chronic pain, chronic disease, etc, etc. The impact of a **No/My** system is catastrophic to our health, and we find, as children it is installed with fear (note it can also be rapidly installed in otherwise intelligent adults, if a threat to life is implied) in the case of wars, terrorism, or a global pandemic emergency. Just a thought…

Henk and I continue…what pattern would you need to have in order for you to remain obedient to the **No/My**? For them to continue applying rules to you that they wouldn't follow themselves. The literature is full of examples of this pattern, Nazi Germany being one of them, where people denied ever being aware of what was happening to the Jews and the atrocities that were being committed. Imagine if that was to happen in your home growing up, how does the cat get your tongue, why won't you yell out, "Enough!"? Well, the answer sits at the feet of one pattern, which is driven by a particular stress response.

There are three basic stress responses fight, flight, or freeze. I'm not going too deep here, I'm working on another book with Mark Johnson that will explain this in minute detail. Flight is the best response. If we run, we can survive. It's a simple process that has allowed evolution to flourish, those who failed to apply the correct process are no longer here. (Check out the dodo for further confirmation).

Fight is the next option. If you can't run, maybe you can fight and win. The problem with either one of these choices is that as a child if the **No/My** is your caregiver you have nowhere to run and you can't fight as they are bigger and stronger. You can't speak out because you might wreck the family home. The option then is the natural adaptive response **FREEZE!** Your mental and physical system clicks into pause. Fight or flight are both fully active processes, they release adrenalin and cortisol, which is burned up in the period that it is activated. Freeze, on the other hand, creates a continuous loop of toxic stress, which impairs our ability to think rationally. If you can't cry out, "The emperor is butt naked!"

From this position of prolonged uncertainty within the *folie en famille*, our system creates the rule structure of compliance; it will naturally delete, distort, and generalise any counter narrative (see Map of the Mind) ensuring your short-term survival. Keep in mind, however, over the medium to long term your mental and physical health is heading to total psychophysiological entropy. The ACEs studies have demonstrated premature mortality of up to 20 years compared to someone without ACEs[94]. The Family Rule structure pattern, by the way, is **Your** rules for me/**Full stop!**

Your/. (Full stop)

> **Your** rules for me/. **(Full stop)**

The pattern of compliance found wherever the No/My is placed in a position of absolute control. They have **Your** rules to apply to themselves **full stop**, period, no matter what.

They are motivated by doing exactly what their master tells them to do.

We've now named the pattern and in Chapter 5 we'll explore it even further. I hope you are as excited as I am.

[94] Brown DW, Anda RF, Tiemeier H, Felitti VJ, Edwards VJ, Croft JB, Giles WH. Adverse childhood experiences and the risk of premature mortality. Am J Prev Med. 2009 Nov;37(5):389-96. doi: 10.1016/j.amepre.2009.06.021. PMID: 19840693.

CHAPTER SUMMARY

In Chapter 4 we looked at how subconscious filters (meta programs) are born out of fear. The fear from our parents as we are about to do something that might hurt us. "Ah!" comes the shout, we stop, we learn, we comply.

We have meta programs for everything that we do. There are 4 meta programs that underlie dis-ease.

ACEs can seriously impact our quality of life, drive psychophysiological dis-ease and shorten our lives by 20 years.

No/My when given absolute power can create Your/.

5

A SLAVE TO THE FAMILY

"Reason enslaves all whose minds are
not strong enough to master her"
George Bernard Shaw

It is late August, 2022. I was sat on the beach today looking for inspiration for this chapter, there are so many examples to encapsulate the Your/. pattern, but which one should I choose, how should I begin? "UUUUuuuurrrr! WAAAAAaaaaggghh!" (I'm not sure if that's how to spell what I heard, just think loud scream) "UUUUuuuurrrr!! WAAAAAaaaaggghh!!!" the sound pierced through me, grabbing my full attention. I turned expecting to see a child being mauled by a hungry lion or attacked by a great white shark. Neither of my instinctive guesses were correct, however, my intuitive connection to the universe supplied me with the beginning of this chapter, how cool.

Whilst Lisa and I were sunbathing, the "Looky, Looky Man" had set up shop. He's the guy who wanders the beaches and the bars selling watches, jewellery, towels, sunglasses, and other trinkets, he always asks you to take a look, hence "Looky, Looky". Today, with the temperature at 28 degrees and full sunshine, he was selling inflatable penguins! The howling that was reverberating along the beach, came from a three year old boy, who was disappointed that the Looky, Looky Man had not given him a penguin. The reason for his cry was not because he had been attacked. However as far as I could tell he was currently running an EMI of a past trauma...Oh yes, this poor little man had suffered similar to this before, and his stress response was on full alert. His face was quivering, he appeared inconsolable, "UUUUuuuurrrrr! WAAAAAaaaaggghh!", "UUUUuuuurrrrr!WAAAAAaaaaggghh!","UUUUuuuurrrrr! WAAAAAaaaaggghh!". The boy had been told "No."

His entire system was falling apart right there in front of us, but he wasn't calling to us for help. The beach was full, where was his parent? Have you ever seen the wildlife documentary when the penguin returns to feed its young (since we're talking about penguins) and there are 50,000 other penguins and their chicks on the beach. Did you wonder how they manage to recognise them? Well, I am not a penguin expert, but I sure as heck know that no one would want to accept responsibility for this child, other than its mother or father. Then the whining stopped abruptly I looked in the direction of the sound machine and out of the ocean of bodies appeared grandma, waving her purse.

This child is three years old and already has absolute power over two generations of the family. As adults, parents, and grandparents Lisa and I were both flabbergasted at the control this little No/My had over his Your/. parents and grandparents. If you pause for a moment, you might just be able to see where My/. could begin to develop within the siblings of this child. His brother or sister, unable to glean any attention from the parents, move more inwardly to exclude the existence of others. Just a thought...

The grandparents have failed their children, their children are failing their children, and the circle of life continues to spiral downwards. Backwards is probably a better word, evolution moves us forwards, we learn, we adapt, we survive, or we thrive. I'd like you to consider for a moment how humanity will be able to thrive if we are already onto third generation Your/. families? What examples of coping with adversity do these children have? The enslaved minds of parents who fail to show, teach, and develop their offspring to be resilient, to bounce back and to rise above adversity. Devolution would appear to be very much on the horizon (did you check out the dodo yet?) The shared intelligence of a group without leadership is likely to be reduced to the lowest denominator or Groupthink.

2+2 = 5 GROUPTHINK

I'm sure that many of you were expecting this chapter to point towards Hitler, Stalin, Lenin, Castro, (insert any current dictatorial leader that may be on the tip of your tongue). We are, instead, looking at the totalitarian regimes that take place in the family, behind closed doors; that is until they are unleashed onto the rest of us!

Encyclopaedia Britannica cites Groupthink as a *mode of thinking in which individual members of small cohesive groups tend to accept a viewpoint or conclusion that represents a perceived group consensus, whether or not the group members believe it to be valid, correct, or optimal. Groupthink reduces the efficiency of collective problem solving within such groups.*[95]

Obviously, 2+2=4. However, if we are isolated, feel personally threatened and are unable to escape or cry out for help, due

---

[95] Schmidt, A. (2016, May 26). *groupthink. Encyclopedia Britannica.* https://www.britannica.com/science/groupthink

to the fact the person or people that we should be able to trust most are the perpetrators. Lifton's work shows us that the group can enter a hypnotic trance as they are brainwashed by the constant narrative. Imagine being that person, child, mother, or father who is locked down inside of this family unit; comply or die would be the mantra running subconsciously inside your mind, being broadcasted across all informational frequencies. If the No/My is allowed full reign, without fear of being caught out or reprimanded then he/she/they will continue to inflict greater and greater pain upon the rest; there will, ironically, be no rest.

My mother would often say "there was no rest for the wicked." She referred to it in the original biblical sense from Isaiah 48:22 'There is *no peace*,' says the Lord, *'for the wicked.'* The wicked soul shall never find rest was the implication of this rule in our family as I grew up. Today the original meaning has been replaced and now points to someone having an unyielding commitment to their work. If my mother was still here, I'm sure she'd still say the original hat fits and should be worn by those for whom it was made. Lifton too, would encourage us to be aware of those who change or attempt to alter the meanings of words, attempting to close our minds to the light of truth.

In her book *Provoked*[96] Kiranjit Ahluwalia shares her harrowing tale of life as a Your/. married to a No/My. Her story emphasises how Groupthink only requires a single authority figure, outside of oneself, to command lower order thinking. Kiranjit arrived in England in 1979 and was placed into an arranged marriage. She was constantly subjected to physical, mental and sexual abuse by her husband. She had no voice, silenced by maintaining the

---

[96] https://www.amazon.com/Provoked-Kiranjit-Ahluwalia-Ahlu-walia-Rahila-Gupta/dp/8172236700

Family Rule - izzat (family honour) "what happens inside the family, remains inside the family", therefore help was never going to arrive. In an interview Kiranjit told the BBC how her husband, Deepak Ahluwalia, grabbed his wife by the hair and branded her, by holding a hot iron on her face. This would prove to be the final straw for Kiranjit.

"I couldn't sleep, I was crying so badly. I was in pain, physically and emotionally," she told the BBC in an interview 30 years later.

"I wanted to hit him. I wanted to hit him the way he hit me. I wanted to hit him so he could feel the same pain I was feeling. I never thought further. My brain had totally stopped."

That night, while he slept in bed, she doused her husband's feet in petrol and set him alight. She grabbed her son and ran out of the house.

"I thought, I'm going to burn his feet, so he won't be able to run after me. I will give him a scar so he will always remember in the end what his wife did to him. So, every time he sees his feet with a scar, he will remember me."[97]

The Your/. had reached the end of the line, enough was enough, 2 + 2 no longer equalled 5, which had been the insane, hypocritical culture of the marital home. She acknowledges that her thinking had stopped. By attacking her ruler, she was breaking the Family Rules. She was supposed to accept and put up with, not anymore. Whatever comes after the deed is done has to be better than doing nothing, there was no need for any more thinking, it was time for her to act and act she did. The only error in her plan was that her actions proved to be fatal, Deepak died 10 days later of his injuries and Kiranjit

---

[97] https://www.bbc.co.uk/news/uk-47724697

was sentenced to life imprisonment for murder. Fortunately, for Kiranjit prison meant safety and freedom from the abuse that she had long suffered. In September 1992 after an appeal a legal precedence was set, the appellant's conviction reduced to manslaughter and Regina v Ahluwalia would stand as a beacon of hope for women in similar situations to gain justice.

The purpose of mentioning the above case is so that we can identify the Family Rule driving the No/my – Your/. relationship. Kiranjit spoke very little English when she arrived in the UK, her family had arranged the marriage, she could not break the izzat. Deepak had no rules for himself and was even having extra marital relationships for which he needed money from his Your/. wife. This is a crucial point. When Deepak begins to spend money on other women, he removes the finance from the family, this loss of funds will impact the mother's children. This, I believe, would have been the point from which our victim would begin to grow a spine, her motivation changed. What would become of her little ones if she allowed this to continue? She could not do this for herself, but she had to do something for them. Burning Deepak's feet would allow her to have some dignity of her own, his feet could be covered up, so that the outside world could not see it. This would stay within the boundaries of the Family Rule. Deepak would have known why his wife had done it, but he too was bound by the same Family Rule, so he would not be able to say anything. For the first time in their marriage, he would be in the same position as his wife; 2+2 = 4. The plan, had it worked, was perfect.

Isolation would appear to be a key component to driving Groupthink, the individual has to sense that they are trapped. Afraid to explore the possibility that the information they are receiving is incorrect or even harmful to them. They join the game of not playing the game.

Unable to flight or fight, the Your/. pattern becomes the best survival mechanism, for now. Allowing abuse to take place time and time again, until one day, SNAP! The camel's back is broken, and justice is served upon those who have been unjust. Deepak believed he was untouchable, he reigned supreme inside the mind of his wife, but as history has shown time and time again, the oppressed eventually rise against their oppressor. I'd recommend *Pedagogy of the Oppressed*[98] by Paulo Freire. It's a classic and has been cited over 106,000 times. Freire encourages us to become interlocutors or partners in the learning process. Within the pages of this book, I hope that you can draw better meanings from the words that I offer you. Meanings with which you can begin to create a better way for you, your family, and the rest of the world.

UNTIL DEATH US DO PART

Although Regina v Ahluwalia had set a legal precedence in English law, it wasn't until 2015 that 'coercive control' (Your/. suffering in No/My environment) a form of domestic abuse, would be seen as a crime. Coercive control is defined perfectly by the organisation Just for Women as: "a way of understanding domestic violence. This foregrounds the psychological abuse and can involve manipulation, degradation, gaslighting (using mind games to make the other person doubt their sanity) and generally monitoring and controlling the person's day-to-day life such as their friends, activities, and clothing. This often leads to the abused becoming isolated and dependent on the abuser"[99]. Although the definition eruditely captures the Your/. living within the No/My environment, the only thing

---

[98] https://daily.jstor.org/paulo-freires-pedagogy-of-the-oppressed-at-fifty/

[99] https://www.justiceforwomen.org.uk/sally-challen-appeal

that I would like to remove is the reference to gender. No/My and Your/. are not automatically assigned gender roles as we shall see later. The universal hold of a Family Rule, however, will still ensnare the senses, and enforce compliance, given the right conditions.

Now for the case of Sally Challen (Your/.) and her husband Richard (No/My). At age 15, still very much a child, Sally met her 22-year-old husband to be. His initial charm faded as nudge by nudge, brick by subconscious brick, he built an invisible wall around his prey.

A 'nudge' used to mean a gentle prod with your elbow to encourage someone to move along. Today, behavioural science uses 'psychological nudging' to influence us in all manner of ways. Richard Thaler and Cass Sunstein popularised this behaviour modification process in their book *Nudge – Improving Decisions about Health, Wealth and Happiness* (2008)[100]. The authors suggested that poor decision making can be influenced or "nudged" to adjust cognitive boundaries, biases or habits so that a person can make a better choice. The key to nudges working well is to ensure that the subject (you or me) is unaware of what is taking place. Think of it as a step-by-step process that can almost guarantee a compliant partner, family, town, country or even a global population. Yes, governments use nudges too, as Laura Dodsworth informs us in her exposé of the inner workings of the UK government. Just imagine a No/My rule structure at the head of government wanting a Your/. population; *A State of Fear: How the UK government weaponised fear during the Covid-19 pandemic*[101], is a compelling read.

---

[100] Thaler, R. H., & Sunstein, C. R. (2008). *Nudge: Improving decisions about health, wealth, and happiness.* Yale University Press.

[101] https://www.amazon.com/State-Fear-government-weaponised-Covid-19/dp/1780667205

Young Sally knew nothing of nudges, but Richard was an accomplished master of them. He chipped away at his spouse's self-esteem and self-worth, controlling every area of her life; her friends and any socialising were monitored by him. The lyrics of The Police song spring to mind "Every breath you take, every move you make, I'll be watching you". Although Sting wrote this to be about a narcissistic, creepy guy (No/My) people think of it as a love song!!!

Richard showed himself to be a true No/My as he partied, had numerous affairs, visited brothels, and flaunted his money. There were no rules for him whilst his wife obeyed all of his rules for her. One could argue that love is blind, deaf, dumb and mute, Sally just loved her man and wanted to be everything for him, she wanted to make him happy. After a short break up, Sally went back to him as she was emotionally crippled without him. She even signed a "post nuptial" agreement that he drew up to prevent her from accessing her correct financial entitlement in the event of a divorce. She also had to agree that she was forbidden to interrupt him or ever speak to strangers. WOW! Just WOW!!

In an interview with Sky news in 2019, her son David said, "You just felt an undercurrent of abuse happening, but you couldn't see the abuse or the moments of it. It was a drip, drip, drip… and that's what my mother suffered behind closed doors," David explained, detailing the decades of coercive control his mother endured.[102]

A short while after they got back together, Richard's behaviour had grown increasingly worse, if that was possible. He sent Sally out into the pouring rain to get his lunch. While she was

---

[102] https://news.sky.com/story/sally-challens-story-driven-to-murder-after-years-of-abuse-11553940

out, he called a woman from a dating agency, who he was planning on meeting. SNAP! Somewhere inside, Sally broke. The man of her dreams was an illusion and the veil fell from her eyes. She couldn't go on another day, another second, the thought of keeping him to herself consumed her $2 + 2 = 5$. All of these years she had attempted to reconcile this equation inside her mind.

Richard was oblivious to the fear defence cascade that was unravelling inside Sally's mind, he provoked her even further by demanding/commanding his subject to be silent. Just like Deepak and so many other tyrannical leaders throughout history, who thought that they could rule supremely forever, judgement day had arrived. As Richard bent forward to eat the breakfast made by his wife, she grabbed a nearby hammer and hit him 20 times.

Sally then stuffed a tea towel in his mouth and wrapped him in old curtains.

Before turning to do the dishes, she wrote a note - 'I love you, Sally' - and placed it on the body, detailed their son David to the reporters in 2019.

On the 14th of August, 2010, 56 year old Sally took a hammer and repeatedly attacked Richard 20 times. She killed him. "Until death do us part," a Family Rule that would allow the mental equation to add up correctly for the first time in their long relationship $2 + 2 = 4$. The following day she travelled to Beachy Head, where she consciously intended to take her own life. One might argue that the subconscious Family Rules about 'being there for her children' or 'always being a good mother' may have overruled her proposed plan.

Sally was convicted of murder and sentenced to life imprisonment, she would serve 9 years and 4 months. After a groundbreaking appeal that highlighted the coercive control she lived under, her sentence was reduced to manslaughter. On 7th June 2019, Sally Challen was formerly released from prison. Yet, she has never been fully released from her relationship with Richard, explains their son David in the interview, "She still loves him and that sounds bizarre but that's coercive control. She was designed to love one man from the age of 15 to 56. It's deep." This emotional connection is not as unusual as you might think, and it has a name - Stockholm syndrome.

STOCKHOLM SYNDROME

Encyclopaedia Britannica[103] defines Stockholm syndrome: psychological response wherein a captive begins to identify closely with his or her captors, as well as with their agenda and demands. It's fascinating to discover that this condition appears to immerge from hostages or victims who have had their life threatened by the wrongdoer. This would create the No/My – Your/. conversion that we have been discussing above. The victims, having been isolated for a period (two days is enough), being made to fear for their lives, then feel they owe their lives to the perpetrators. It's as though the victims enter a trance state and fail to accept what has happened to them is wrong.

What would happen if these innocent people were coerced into believing that their lives were in mortal danger and were forced to isolate from everyone for a couple of weeks, with nothing but their captors face and voice being fed into their

[103] Lambert, Laura. "Stockholm syndrome". Encyclopedia Britannica, 22 Aug. 2022, https://www.britannica.com/science/Stockholm-syndrome. Accessed 28 August 2022.

home. Stockholm Syndrome By Proxy, or as Mattias Desmet, Professor of Psychology at Ghent University, explains *Mass Formation*[104]. Curiously, even though many psychologists recognise Stockholm syndrome and there is a plethora of incidents where it has been cited, the American Psychiatric Association does not include Stockholm syndrome in its Diagnostic and Statistical Manual of Mental Disorders (DSM). Strange.

Had Stockholm syndrome been added to the DSM it would have made it easier for the legal teams of Kiranjit Ahluwalia, Sally Challen and countless others to defend their Your/. clients. If we put ourselves in the judge's position in the original trials, we would have heard how both women had been subjected to immense abuse over a period of years; but where is the motive for carrying out the attack on their husbands in this specific instance? The answer then was none. Both women had suffered at the hand of their husbands, yet at no point did they lash out, maim, or hurt their perpetrators. We must ask ourselves what was the specific reason that drove each of these otherwise gentle souls to commit such violent acts? Back then, not being made aware of Stockholm syndrome or coercive control, I'm afraid that we might also have to judge the defendants as murderers.

When we use the Family Rules to filter information, both women became wives and mothers. As we shall see in the next chapter, identity comes with a certain set of rules built in. Marriage, for example may imply "until death do we part." Neither of the defendants wished to kill their husbands, but they did want to be treated better. Family Rules around marriage and being a good wife, to love, honour and obey, for

---

[104] https://www.amazon.com/Psychology-Totalitarianism-Mattias-Desmet/dp/1645021726

richer, for poorer, in sickness and in health. That's quite a lot of rules to follow, and in a My/My relationship it's plausible. However, inside of a No/My relationship this can only force the other spouse (male or female) into enslavement.

In Kiranjit's case her attempt to draw a line under her husband's Your/. rule after 10 years, ended with his accidental death. In Sally's case after serving 41 years of loyal devotion to her despotic No/My husband, in a split-second her survival mechanism switched from the near lifetime of freeze to fight! It was in this moment of pure rage that Sally's primitive brain unleashed the wrath of hell upon her captor, jailer, master. We must understand that Family Rules will remain in place right up until the point that they are no longer tenable. This is how I would serve Sally's defence today, and all of those other Your/.'s (male or female) who, with nowhere else to turn, snap! Perhaps, the action taken to terminate the No/My-Your/. contract is best identified in the words of Martin Luther King, Jr., in his letter from Birmingham jail, "One has not only a legal but a moral responsibility to obey just laws. Conversely, one has a moral responsibility to disobey unjust laws."[105]

PLEASE SIR, CAN I HAVE SOME MORE?

The No/My pattern has a tried and tested approach when it comes to creating Your/. (Remember Lifton's Thought Reform process in Chapter 3.) This game of manipulation has gone on since the dawn of time. As soon as you view the world through these filters they are everywhere.

---

[105] https://www.africa.upenn.edu/Articles_Gen/Letter_Birmingham.html

Take William (Bill) Sykes, the fictional character and main antagonist in Charles Dickens 1838 classic novel Oliver Twist, for example. Although a member of Fagin's gang, Sykes is an absolute No/My, a vicious, evil man who drives fear into all of those around him. There is a horrific scene where his partner, Nancy, is bludgeoned to death by Sykes, after he finds out that she has informed the police about him. After killing Nancy, Sykes gathers some rocks, ties them together and calls to his dog Bullseye.

Dickens shows us that he has an exquisite insight into the No/ My – Your/. psyche. This scene, for me personally, depicts how an animal is able to unlearn the Your/. rule of subservience, compliance, and submission, in a split-second. Sykes knows that the police will be looking for a man with a white dog, he can take no chances, his faithful dog has to die too. Bullseye has witnessed the murder of Nancy and understands fully what the weighted rope is for. As Sykes calls his dog to come to heel, near the water's edge, Bullseye freezes and within a moment Snap! Bullseye runs from the scene, to bring help for young Oliver and judgement for his master. In director David Lean's 1948 adaptation the camera focuses on Bullseye, scratching frantically at the door in a desperate attempt to escape the barbaric scene. This lays the groundwork for the mental shift inside the dog. If you get the chance to watch the 1968 'Oliver' movie also, you can make your own comparison. The 1968 version stars Oliver Reed who immortalised the role of Bill Sykes.

Did you know that scholars and critics have dismissed the Nancy murder scene as over the top. In fact, many film adaptations cut the scene back from the gruesome, grisly, scene that Dickens work depicts. It wasn't until 2009 that Rebecca Gowers, a freelance journalist and writer, presented compelling evidence that the scene was based on a real murder.

The case of Eliza Grimwood was one of the best-known of all Victorian murders. When the Jack the Ripper murders started 50 years later the Daily Telegraph said, "If you want to know how ghastly these Whitechapel murders are, they are as bad as the Grimwood murder," said Gowers. "In the 19th century the murder was totemic, it was absolutely one of the key cases in the cultural imagination.[106]"

The impact of trauma that left Marcus looking older than his unknowing twin in Chapter 2, also highlights the impact that the No/My-Your/. relationship can have on our physical system. As Gower points out, the murder scene was one of Dickens favourites. In order to get this scene perfect, the writer needed to have many interviews with the police officers and detectives that had first-hand knowledge of such crimes. It's therefore possible that Dickens brought about his own death by holding this information within his mind, thus accelerating his entropic demise. In any event his close friends blamed his vigorous re-enactment of the Sykes scene for causing him to have a stroke at age 58. Who knew?

Just to bring a little bit of light-heartedness to this chapter, I stumbled on an episode of Doctor Who called "The God Complex" in the BBC series. The actor David Walliams plays the fictional character 'Gibbis' a submissive mole (Your/.) from the planet Tivoli – the most invaded planet in the universe, whose national anthem is called 'Glory to (insert here)'- meaning they have been oppressed so many times by different No/My's, their anthem is interchangeable. The Doctor points

---

[106] https://www.theguardian.com/books/2009/apr/11/dickens-oli-ver-twist-eliza-grimwood-murder

out that the Tivolian civilisation is one of the oldest in the galaxy, because they are insanely submissive and willing to comply. "Their cowardice", the doctor notes "is not quaint it's sly, aggressive". With this chapter in mind, it's worth a watch.

THE MILGRAM EXPERIMENT

History is littered with Your/.'s who are willing to go to any lengths to satisfy their No/My master's bidding. Think Myra Hindley[107]or Rose West[108], both took part in horrific crimes at the behest of their No/My partners.

Did you know that our need to obey authority has already been tried and tested? In 1974 social psychologist, Stanley Milgram set up an experiment[109] whereby individuals had to administer an electric current to another person. The process was rigged so the dosage would not exceed the safe level and kill the recipient of the electrical dose. Obviously, no one was hurt, Milgram had an actor play the recipient of the electrical current and the electrical current never exceeded 45 volts, it was set low so the actor knew when to pretend they were being shocked.

On the surface the experiment sounded straight forward, the volunteers thought they were helping in a study to see the effects of punishment on learning ability. Each time the learner got a question wrong, they would be zapped, and the current would incrementally increase. The participants believed that they too could be in the learner's chair and

---

[107] https://www.biography.com/crime-figure/myra-hindley
[108] https://www.nationalworld.com/news/crime/where-is-rose-west-now-story-of-serial-killer-wife-of-fred-west-3241113
[109] Milgram, S. (1974). *Obedience to Authority: An Experimental View.* New York: Harper and Row.

receive the same treatment, but this step was omitted from the experiment without their knowledge. They would remain in the position of "Teacher" giving the punishment and not "Student" receiving it.

Just pause for a moment and take this in!

The whole set up was designed to make it very clear what the teacher was doing. Shock levels were labelled with a numerical scale from 15 to 450 volts. Above each number, the jolt levels had verbal anchors labelled: "slight shock," "moderate shock," "strong shock," "very strong shock," "intense shock," and "extreme intensity shock." The last two were "Danger: Severe Shock," and, beyond this point it just had a terrifying "XXX."

The actor playing the student had a script to follow; 75 volts - groan, 120 volts - complain, 150 volts - ask to be released. After this point increase the amount of protesting and begin screaming in agony at 285 volts. From this point the student had to complain that they were having heart problems. If the student was silent the teacher was to take this as noncompliance and increase the voltage. Then between 330 volts and 450 volts, the actor is deadly silent. From 450 volts it was abundantly clear that the student would be killed by the teacher. When the teachers hesitated, they were told "The experiment *requires* that you continue." Perhaps detaching the human element and saying "The experiment requires" influenced the motivation of the teacher to comply, in an "It's for the greater good" sort of way. In any case, Milgram was shocked at the results. How many teachers do you think refused to go ahead? Milgram had anticipated that the majority of people would question the authority of the experiment and call a halt to the proceedings very early on, but he was wrong. Sixty-five percent of the teachers were willing to take innocent students up to 450 volts, or in other words they killed them!

The study participants had acted in the same way as many of the doctors and nurses who had carried out barbaric human rights violations under the Nazis. The experiment encompassed the work of Lifton, which we read in Chapter 3, and concluded that teachers would obey authority so long as they felt (1) the authority figure was close by; (2) teachers felt they could pass on responsibility to others; and (3) experiments took place under the auspices of a respected organisation. Who knew?

Let's have a look at this form of obedience as a child, from within the family context; (1) Mum, Dad, Caregiver - the authority figure is close; (2) Parents/caregivers under stress may externalise and blame others; (3) As a child, the family is the only organisation that commands our respect. If you've ever seen the movie or read the book[110] 'The Godfather' then you'll know what I'm talking about. Without a direct challenge to the harmful authority, the experiment becomes a delusional process shared by the volunteer and the experimenter close association; a *folie à deux*, as Lidz informed us earlier.

From here it becomes a little easier to see how a small group may enter *folie en famille: characterized as a shared psychotic disorder within a family in more than two members. The involved patients have an unusually close relationship and are isolated from others*[111]. What if we were to take this a step further? By and large we are governed by a paternal system: *a system under which an authority undertakes to supply needs or regulate conduct*

[110] https://www.amazon.com/Godfather-Signet-Mario-Puzo/dp/0451167716
[111] Srivastava A, Borkar HA. Folie a famille. Indian J Psychiatry. 2010 Jan;52(1):69-70. doi: 10.4103/0019-5545.58899. PMID: 20174522; PMCID: PMC2824986.

of those under its control in matters affecting them as individuals as well as in their relations to authority and to each other[112]. What if our paternal rulers, prime ministers, governments, and authorities begin to enforce Draconian rules upon us, the family members of society? If we the people allowed our governments to apply rules to us and not to themselves, we have the potential for 'folie en Société' or "Mass Formation," as Desmet informs us[113]. A No/My at the head of society has the potential for a society wide Your/., a delusional trance state that may never be noticed; the household Family Rules become a global destructive groupthink. Just a thought…

Getting back to Milgram, the conclusion he reached was that people obey for two reasons: fear or the desire to please; even when they were going against their own beliefs. Milgram placed the behaviours of the participants into three categories:

Obeyed but justified themselves. Obedient participants externalised responsibility for their actions and blamed the experimenter. If the learner was harmed then it would be the experimenter's fault, not theirs. Others blamed the learner: "He was so stupid and stubborn he deserved to be shocked."

Obeyed but blamed themselves. These individuals beat themselves up over their failure to say enough and to stop the process, which was leading to people's deaths. Hopefully these people would remember in the future and wake up if anything like this were to happen again!

Rebelled. The rebellious group although in the minority, showed hope for humanity. As these individuals were able to recognise when human rights were being violated. They

---

[112] https://www.merriam-webster.com/dictionary/paternalism

[113] https://www.amazon.com/Psychology-Totalitarianism-Mattias-Desmet/dp/1645021726

argued for a greater ethical perspective to protect the needs of the learner. Some of these participants felt

they were accountable to a higher authority and not the 'greater good' that the experiment implied.

As I read the categories above, I have mixed emotions. Yes, I am very happy to know which group I fit in with. But at the same time, right now I know there are many people around the world who fall into the obedient categories, which is chilling. No wonder the actor Keanu Reeves said, "The Matrix is not a movie, it's a documentary." Reeves, who plays Neo, the chosen one who has come to save us all from the machines, is reminded by his mentor, Morpheus, that anyone who isn't unplugged is a potential agent. By Milgram's calculations, 35% of us are awake and fully aware of what is happening in the world right now. Does that include you? If not, then I suggest you remember your ancestors were fighters, you are born from a line of warriors, not worriers!

The takeaway from this chapter for us should be that many of us want to trust all is well in the world. If we believe this, then our stress system remains deactivated, leaving us to live long, healthy, and happy lives. However, if this is not the case, it may be time to realise that 65% of the population will be Your/. if they have a No/My in power. The same Your/.'s will be reluctant to confront those who abuse their power, so learning more about the impact of Family Rules is essential for humanity. The No/My can only remain in power with the Your/.'s permission. It was too late for Nancy, who died at the hands of Sykes, but the spirit of Kiranjit Ahluwalia and Sally Challen arose, bringing a swift end to tyrannical rulers. The No/My knows this only too well and that is why there can be no peace for the wicked. One might begin to wonder what may happen in the U.K. now that another No/My resides at number 10 Downing Street. Will it be mass compliance a *"folie en Société"* or do we cry *"Enough!"*.

CHAPTER SUMMARY

In this chapter we've learned that subconscious filters play a key role in compliance. Specifically, No rules for me/My rules for You and Your rules for me/Full stop (period).

The Your/. relationship can be found anywhere that someone has power or influence and abuses it. People who run No/My create Your/.'s within the home, the office and even society.

No/My's can drive groupthink as others within the group are afraid to speak out, silenced by the fear of being expelled from or punished by the group. Rishi Sunak for example has just announced that he knew that the British government have been using behavioural psychology to terrorise the population into compliance. One wonders if it was groupthink that tied his tongue then and what has changed today, or rather who has given him permission to speak? Read the full article in the Spectator[114].

Family Rules can lock us into a particular way of being until it is untenable.

Family Rules point to the specific motivational triggers for stress responses, i.e., fight, flight, and freeze. When those circumstances change then Snap! The sheep becomes the lion.

Stockholm syndrome clearly shows the relationship between No/My and Your/.

---

[114] https://www.spectator.co.uk/article/the-lockdown-files-rishi-sunak-on-what-we-werent-told/

Obedience accounts for 65% of the population and they may well kill if instructed to do so.

A person who falls into the game can become a compliant Your/. a slave or even a collaborator. Remember the people who hid Anne Frank were breaking the law and the people who turned her in were following it[115].

[115] https://www.annefrank.org/en/

6

RELATIONSHIP RULES
AND FILTERS

"Treasure your relationships,
not your possessions."
Anthony J. D'Angelo

In her book *The New PeopleMaking*, Virginia Satir asks us to consider sameness and difference when it comes to relationships. Virginia, believed that it is our similarities that initially bring us together, we seek a connection, some way of saying to ourselves we are one and the same. However, she adds that in order for a relationship to continue over the long-term then differences need to be appreciated too.

Relationships sit at the heart of Family Rules, as we shall no doubt discover on our journey. I hope that you and I are getting along. I'm enjoying sharing my world with you and sincerely wish that you can awaken fully to the beauty of the world around you.

Within the meta programs of NLP there are 3 filters for relationships: Sameness, Evolution and Difference. I'll explain each of them in turn and then you can figure out who's who in your relationships with family and friends.

SAMENESS

Wants the world to stay the same, 15 to 25 year clock.

"It's the same as always," "There is no need to change what I'm doing," "We always do it this way," "That's just the way I am."
Notice only what is the same or familiar when the experience changes. They will strongly resist change, reject anything different or new (in the context).
Unable to adapt when change is forced on them - they usually experience dis-stress. Influence them with "it will be the same as your content…" "See how similar it is?" "it's identical to.." "just as we always do." "totally familiar," "we'll maintain the status quo."

EVOLUTION

The Evolution filter has 2 steps in it: Step 1 Sameness with Evolution and Step 2 Difference with Evolution. It makes logical sense as we glide from the traditional mindset, which is similar to the improved yet radical view. If we check the last sentence we can see how we have travelled from sameness, sameness with evolution, difference with evolution to difference. The changes are subtle, but they are also key to communicating across the void, we call reality.

Sameness with Evolution:
Wants evolution, 5 to 7 year clock.

Difference with Evolution:
Likes change, comfortable with evolution, 2 to 3 year clock.

DIFFERENCE

From an evolutionary perspective difference means danger. If our ancestors were out hunting for food and there was something different in that environment, a scent or large paw prints they didn't recognise, their defence system would be on high alert. Today we may not have the same predators chasing us, but we are still hard wired for changes in our environment. People with the difference filter, crave this and are motivated to find it or create a revolution to cause it. This may go a long way to explaining why Sameness and Difference rub each other up the wrong way, oil and water don't mix.

Needs revolution, 12 to 18 months clock. "It's totally new / different / unique / always / changing" Make sense of the world by noticing what is different and have a high need for change. As innovators they resist anything that hasn't changed in some way or is considered fixed or inflexible.

Because they notice *and comment on* what is different or out of place, they may be perceived as critical. They may not understand the 'relationship' question in the context where they filter for differences and in extreme cases may mismatch others. Influence with "It's totally different," "It's new, revolutionary, cutting edge," "fast paced" "Always changing," "you'll love the variety."

WHAT DO THE CLOCK TIMES MEAN?

Although they may appear self-explanatory the 'clock times' connected to the relationship filters are definitely worth noticing. As we discovered in the last chapter when it's time to change, we change. The subconscious itch that has driven you to read this book, seek out help for your relationship or assist you to have a relationship for more than 2 months, may be sitting inside this chapter. Let's hope so.

Consider for a moment beginning a 15 to 25 year commitment today. Did you just take a deep breath in and feel a cold chill run down your back? That's your entire system saying NO! It could also be the size of the commitment you've made inside your mind; 25 years can look like a huge wall, cage, or mountain. The sameness filter will make this passage of time smaller as you go forwards and larger as you look back. Hence, some people get trapped in relationships because they look at the years they've had together as a huge investment. Nobody likes to lose a huge investment, so they stay and grumble along until death; or they inject more difference into the relationship to stoke the coals or reignite the fire that once burned without needing attention.

When the English songwriter Michael James Hucknall (Mick Hucknall) wrote the lyrics to *Holding Back the Years* he was 17 years old, yet the words have the depth that is required of any classic song. Mick was 25 when his band Simply Red[116] released it as part of their debut album in 1985. What do you notice as you read the words, maybe it's better to pop it into YouTube and listen to it for full effect.

Holding back the years
Thinking of the fear I've had so long
When somebody hears
Listen to the fear that's gone
Strangled by the wishes of pater
Hoping for the arms of mater
Get to me the sooner or later

I'll keep holding on
I'll keep holding on

Holding back the years
Chance for me escape from all I've known
Holding back the tears
Cause nothing here has grown
I've wasted all my tears
Wasted all those years
Nothing had the chance to be good
Nothing ever could, yeah, ah oh oh oh

Hucknall's mum left him and his dad when he was 3 years old, does knowing this give you a different context to filter with? He was holding back the future when he wrote this, he

---

[116] http://www.simplyred.com/home/

didn't want tomorrow to come, at age 17 the big wide world was calling. The fears and the Family Rules of father and mother are both on display. How many of us have wondered if we have wasted all those years, if that's you then you can tick the sameness box. Could it be yours is the only filter that will amass that length of time? Nope, others may still be in long-term relationships, and get their difference filter fulfilled elsewhere, maybe you move house or job every 7 years. Each move will reset your clock.

Family Rules are soaked in tradition and extend way beyond 25 years, they are unknowingly handed down through generations. If your parents took you to school and they shrank as they approached other parents in the queue to drop you off, you learnt something. Would that learning cause you to shrink (Away From) or drive you to grow (Towards). What messages did you hear from your parents and how did you translate them? Mick Hucknall, (chose towards) like so many others came from a one parent home, or some may say a "broken home." What Family Rules may be born out of this gap, or drawn out of this nothing, this empty space. How does the remaining parent fill the void, do they overcompensate or avoid all talk of the deserter; shutting you down as if mother, father, mummy, or daddy are blasphemous words, never to be uttered. There would certainly be an impact on how or if, you would ever get into a relationship. Perhaps, you too may be holding back the years, hoping to avoid commitment, but how much is it costing, or what has it cost you so far?

THE PRICE OF COMMITMENT

Allow me to introduce you to Miss P who was similar to J who we met in Chapter 2. Miss P had a problem around commitment, she was trapped in a Family Rule of 'Until death us do part' (sameness). She was a difference child born into a sameness family, a cuckoo in the nest. She, too, was holding back the years, afraid like Hucknall of the future. But Miss P had a high Away From pattern, which held her trapped as a teenager and she was almost 40. Her parents' relationship terrified her, "It just goes on and on for eternity," she explained. (There's your Difference relationship filter alert). Miss P did not want to have the same life as her mother, "You want yours to be different" I interjected "Yes! Totally!" she replied, excited because she felt heard. I knew Miss P was operating from a difference filter. Before she spoke, by the way, she arrived in khaki trousers, black, military-style boots, a dye wash t-shirt, a nose piercing, and dyed red hair. You don't have to be Sherlock Holmes to do this stuff.

If you have a 'difference filter' you will have grown up with statements like "Where did we get you from?"

"Why can't you be like your brother/sister?"

"Why can't you just do as you're told?"

"Why do you have to be so different?" As you hear these statements you can either shrink or grow as the Family Rule pulls you down or raises you up. Maybe your parents would project their own anger onto you as they failed to understand that you weren't like them. You were at the opposite end of the relationship motivational pool. This didn't mean that you were actually angry, although it might frustrate you a lot as they try to give you a guilt sandwich with the "You disappoint me" routine.

The subconscious mind plays a huge role in our lives from this perspective. We know we have to align with the Family Rules as children in order to survive, but what happens to our chances of thriving when we are the cuckoo in the nest? We can either flourish in the positive attention from our parents/caregivers, flourish in the negative attention from them, or the subconscious Family Rules become like kryptonite, draining our energy and blocking our development, full stop, period. $2 + 2 = 5$.

Miss P had paid the price of commitment by not committing to herself. A tiny-framed dormouse of what could be a woman sat before me. She'd never managed to hold down a relationship with any eligible partner. She always chose to play it safe by having affairs with married men or hooking up with the occasional lunatic for short periods of unsatisfying sex, with zero intimacy. Forty was knocking on her door, it was time. All the while she was running from the commitment she had made to herself about never committing to a relationship like her parents had.

I have a pack of cards that I keep for such occasions (the images that I've used in this book come from this pack). They have all of the meta programs we need to help us update this Family Rule. Maybe I could have used the same process as J but I'm an options kind of guy, so I came up with something different to fit my client's main stumbling block. We needed to integrate and indeed update her view of commitment and sameness. Please note my use of 'We', if I do it then the client will have nothing to hold onto, therefore Miss P must make the journey with me by her side, not in front or behind. "How many years have your parents been married?" I asked, in a just curious kind of way. "42" she replied in a what sort of question is that kind of way. So far so good. The client thinks I'm dumb, wonderful!

I learned long ago, thanks mostly to William Shakespeare, the fool is often overlooked, yet says and knows what others fear to say and know, for fear of reprimand. Neurologically I'm just getting the client to switch off her threat responses on a below conscious level, so that I can step inside her mind, onto her mental map and have her create some changes before she has a chance to notice. ('Sneaky, Mr Hudson', I hear you). "Your mother and father have been committed to each other for 42 years and you've been against commitment for almost 40, give or take?" As I said this I raised both arms, the left to represent the parents and the right to represent Miss P. "More or less," she replied, with her "I have no idea where you are going with this" look. I then studied the difference in height between both commitments, dropping my left arm slightly, I then pointed at the small size which I had made between my thumb and index finger with my right hand. NLP lovers could call this next step a visual squash.

I proceeded to explain that "All of this has mounted up to a tiny piece of that. A piece that has puzzled you all. A peace that any parent would wish for their child. A peace that fits with you and them, you are their piece. They know that you are different, they just don't have the piece that lets them understand what difference is. All of these years they've never really had this peace and neither had you, up until now. And now what other pieces are you noticing as this peace fills those gaps". I added that last line as I watched Miss P's eyes fill with salt water and dance around from thought to thought. The Family Rule had been upgraded.

In the above paragraph I use piece and peace interchangeably as you can see, however this is not the case in the spoken word, as its meaning can become ambiguous. Milton Erickson called them 'Phonological Ambiguities', they allow the client to fill the meanings for themselves. Do ewe sea what eye mean? I also inflect my voice downwards in a command tone. This helps the subconscious come to heel, remember Ah!, it's very similar, just a lot more trance like. Let's keep in mind that the Family Rule has the client frozen in time, so there is at least one nominalisation present. This information tells us that the freeze response is engaged whenever the client gets close to the context. Hence, none of the paragraph pertains to the presenting problem.

We begin with a generalisation 'All' then we associate the 'All' by adding 'this', so 'All of this' leaves space for the mind to fill the gap because the subject matter has been deleted. Whatever the deleted subject matter is, there is a lot of it because it 'has mounted up'. Then comes the apposition of opposites another of Erickson's brilliant hypnotic language patterns, which encompasses the whole sentence 'All of this has mounted up' directing the clients mind to a large associated something then we switch mid-sentence to point the client in the opposite direction making the something tiny whilst disassociating from it with the use of 'that'. There is of course the use of presuppositional language to further embed the sentence and the actions required by the listener.

The paragraph above gives you a tiny indication as to what is going on when I approach a Family Rule. It took all of the paragraph to explain 10 words that form one sentence in my session with Miss P. There is obviously a lot more to this than meets the eye, or the ear for that matter. I just thought I would let you see a sample of my work so you can get the gist. It can be difficult to follow when looking in from the outside. It's great fun when a client feeds back "You're useless", "You only chatted with me", or best of all "You never did anything!" only to find a few days or weeks later that their lifelong problem has disappeared. It's not called subconscious change for nothing..! Anyway, back to Miss P.

We sat for a few minutes in silence, as her mind worked in hyperdrive to create a whole, where there was once a hole. "What just happened?" she enquired. "Not a clue Miss P" I shrugged. "It's Penelope" she beamed. In a follow up session Penelope had stepped into her new role. The adult who she had feared to become and fought so hard not to be, was now the person she loved. Physically, mentally, and visibly she had transformed. 2 + 2 = 4.

YOU'VE MADE YOUR BED, YOU'LL LIE IN IT

There are as many Family Rules as there are situations for us to enter. Below conscious gate keepers of identity, but who's identity? Is it yours, your parents or even your grandparents who have passed this on, unknowingly, unwittingly, like an asymptomatic virus. They don't know they have it, but it leaves its mark, tampering with your DNA and impacting your life choices. This particular rule we are putting under the microscope is heard and used in everyday parlance. It seems fair enough on the surface, if you have gone to the trouble of making your own bed, then I'm sure you will intend to sleep in it at some stage in the next 24 hours or so.

The logical surface layer is not what it may seem, as we travel underneath to feel the grip of its bind. The unconscious leash tightening around our throats, choking us until we yield and obey. Did you ever consider that the speaker of the sentence commands that the listener 'must lie in it' using a downward inflection in the tone of their voice. Hmmm…I'm sure I've mentioned that voice inflection earlier, maybe you can remember? If you can remember then this particular Family Rule has no hold over you. If you can't it may mean an embedded command already has a hold on you. An 'embedded command' is a way of saying something to someone's subconscious mind, that will enhance the chance the listener will comply with your request. It can be used positively by a professional to whom you have given permission to alter your thoughts, or negatively, nudge after psychological nudge, day after day from those who tell us they care yet show us they don't. Five points if you've just thought No/My has a hand in this Family Rule, but we need to go deeper, deeper and deeper. What pattern does the enforcer of the rule need, in order to ensure that it is adhered to?

At various points during our journey, we have seen the No/My at the centre of human atrocities, both in the family and in the world at large, however this particular Family Rule does not need a No/My to enforce it. In a twisted way the rule structure **My** rules for me/**My** rules for you (My/My) (See Chapter 4) is the greatest executioner of this Draconian rule. Draco was an Athenian lawgiver in Ancient Greece, his laws were severe and cruel and inflicted heavy punishments on small offences[117]. My/My's are very comfortable with life just the way it is!

You may even hear them use the phrase "That's just how it is" or "It is what it is" These will give you a very large insight into who the 'hatchet person' is, hopefully before they deliver the blow to cut off your head or report you to the state as they did in Nazi Germany. After all, if the state decapitates you or enslaves you, then you obviously deserved to be punished. "Why don't you just do as you are told!" the My/My will exclaim, but you will not yield. You cannot surrender to Draco because you have already surrendered to a higher spiritual cause. A sense of purpose that the My/My cannot share, for if he/she opened their mind then their greatest fear would be unleashed. If you read Chapter 4, you'll know what I am

---

[117] Draconian Laws. (n.d.) *West's Encyclopedia of American Law, edition 2*. (2008). Retrieved September 1 2022 from https://legaldictionary.thefreedictionary.com/Draconian+Laws

about to say, the greatest living nightmare for a My/My is CHANGE!! They would sooner die than have to face it.

Now that we've uncovered the type of mindset that is needed to maintain this Family Rule, make no bones about it, their mind is definitely set. Let's see what else we can reveal from the words 'must lie in it'. 'Must' is a modal operator of necessity (Chapter 1 remember?) so you have to obey, you need to obey. If you are okay being told what to do and how to think, then 'must' will be easy for you to deal with, for the rest of us, it's a problem. A problem that can create psychophysiological dis-ease within those who push back against it.

The next word following 'must' is 'lie'. 'Must lie' so, you are going to have to keep on telling lies to yourself and others if you are going to make this relationship last. Do you detect a conflict here? Usually, a parent raises their child to tell the truth, yet here they are plainly and clearly commanding them to lie; to 'lie in it'. The 'it' is a deletion filter alert, what is 'it'? Clearly 'it' is whatever subject matter or context the speaker sees fit to imply, marriage, relationship, even your career choice. This Family Rule is rolled out whenever a person who feels trapped or imprisoned begins to show signs of going over the wall! Ah! Stop! "The grass is always greener on the other side, but it still needs mowing!" the My/My jailer chips in, never realising that he too is a slave in Plato's allegoric cave.

Indeed, it was Plato[118] who truly shone light on this condition humans are apt to suffer from. The My/My filter allows a person to believe the reality that is presented to them without the need for critical thinking. These 'prisoners' Plato tells us, would mistake what appeared to them as reality, to be reality. The prisoners would talk about the shadows on the T.V. as if

---

[118] https://faculty.washington.edu/smcohen/320/cave.htm

they were real. They would never consider the agenda behind the shadows, the covert intended meanings or behavioural nudges on the 'tell lie vision'. There is a lot to absorb from Plato's ancient wisdom, that fits with the clearance of Family Rules. However, those who made the rules, then and now, were not happy at the thought of their prisoners waking up to the game that was being played upon them.

Another reason the My/My demands 'you must lie in it' is because he or she has signed up to the same fate. They are already in 'it' so if they can, you can (My/My). It really does sound reasonable, but they are not offering, they are telling, and they require us to keep the lie going about 'it'! The biggest problem with lies, is that it has to be covered with other lies and so the game begins. What sets us all free from a big fat lie or even a string of lies? The bible has a word or two to say about the truth – 'and you will know the truth, and the truth will set you free[119]' The truth, however blindingly obvious it may appear to you, does not necessarily equal the truth for the person who is suffering with this particular Family Rule. Remember The Map of The Mind in Chapter 2, their system will delete, distort, and generalise any information that challenges the status-quo.

A CHEMICAL IMBALANCE IN THE BRAIN

How many people do you know who use antidepressants or alcohol to get through their day? Many is a reasonable answer. Since the early 90s doctors have been diagnosing mental health conditions e.g., depression as a 'chemical imbalance' in the brain. This pervasive myth was spread far and wide

---

[119] John 8:32 The Bible

by physicians, pharmaceutical companies, and the media. Allegedly 'serotonin' was to blame.

Serotonin is a chemical that carries messages between nerve cells in the brain and throughout your body. Serotonin plays a key role in body functions such as mood, sleep, digestion, nausea, wound healing, bone health, sexual desire, and blood clotting in the coronary disease population[120]. With serotonin playing a role in all of the neurophysiological functions, it would obviously make sense that influencing this chemical would have an impact on our mood, right? The 'cause' of the problem had been identified and the pharmaceutical industry had manufactured a treatment to coincide with the research. Selective serotonin reuptake inhibitors (SSRIs) hit the market. The UK National Health Service (NHS) website has this to say on the subject:

"After carrying a message, serotonin is usually reabsorbed by the nerve cells (known as "reuptake"). SSRIs work by blocking ("inhibiting") reuptake, meaning more serotonin is available to pass further messages between nearby nerve cells."[121] The media and the health service make a compelling argument for why we should take the drug, but is there any real scientific evidence?

The 'chemical imbalance' idea has recently been put under close scrutiny; researchers wanted to know is it true?

---

[120] Sanner JE, Frazier L. The role of serotonin in depression and clotting in the coronary artery disease population. J Cardiovasc Nurs. 2011 Sep-Oct;26(5):423-9. doi: 10.1097/JCN.0b013e3182076a81. PMID: 21372736.

[121] https://www.nhs.uk/mental-health/talking-therapies-medi-cine-treatments/medicines-and-psychiatry/ssri-antidepressants/overview/#:~:text=It's%20thought%20to%20have%20a,mes-sages%20between%20nearby%20nerve%20cells.

Surveys have indicated that over 80% of the public believe that depression is caused by a 'chemical imbalance'[122] as do many general practitioners (GPs)[123]. In March 2022, Joanna Moncrieff and her team of researchers published the results of a systematic umbrella review, taken from the past 2 decades, for *the serotonin theory of depression*. The verdict was: "The main areas of serotonin research provide no consistent evidence of there being an association between serotonin and depression, and no support for the hypothesis that depression is caused by lowered serotonin activity or concentrations. Some evidence was consistent with the possibility that long-term antidepressant use reduces serotonin concentration.[124]"

Perhaps, it's time to recognise the impact trauma has on us. From early childhood to now, the impact of adverse events gnaw away at us; reducing our energy and connection to others as we endure psychophysiological entropy.

Why is a book about Family Rules informing you of corruption and collusion between the pharmaceutical industry, media and the health service? This is to demonstrate to you that No/My resides at a higher societal level and its pervasive influence require Your/. and/or My/My to do its bidding. Take a few moments and allow this to sink in. Family Rules are institutionalised and permeate across the world, is it any

---

[122] Pilkington PD, Reavley NJ, Jorm AF. The Australian public's beliefs about the causes of depression: associated factors and changes over 16 years. J Affect Disord. 2013;150:356–62.

[123] Read J, Renton J, Harrop C, Geekie J, Dowrick C. A survey of UK general practi- tioners about depression, antidepressants and withdrawal: implementing the 2019 Public Health England report. Therapeutic Advances in. Psychopharmacology. 2020;10:204512532095012.

[124] Moncrieff, J., Cooper, R.E., Stockmann, T. *et al.* The serotonin theory of depression: a systematic umbrella review of the evidence. *Mol Psychiatry* (2022). https://doi.org/10.1038/s41380-022-01661-0

wonder that poor mental health is the real pandemic. Just a thought…

CHANGE IS TO BE FEARED, NOT WELCOMED:
SAMENESS AND EVOLUTION

Steven and Denise came for their session together. Denise had called to make an appointment for her husband of 18 years, he had developed agonising pains in his legs. The pain started a couple of years ago and was intermittent. Now his condition had become chronic, and his GP had suggested he see me. I am always intrigued when an adult gets someone else to make the appointment, is the client being sent or are they attending of their own free will? Steven, as it turned out, was keen to rid himself of the chronic pain he was suffering. He had been in the same job for 25 years, travelling to work each day on his bicycle (a 10 mile round trip). "When I'm cycling I'm okay, it's just when I stop" he explained, to a chap who must have looked as though he was listening, but I wasn't. I was fascinated by something much bigger than Steven's legs, 2 + 2 = 5; his whole demeanour was sameness. He was a straightforward, time-served engineer, who worked for the same company that took him on at age 16. A black and white no colour, measured individual, just a plain unassuming, steady, nice guy. He spoke in monotone in a measured way, and I liked him instantly.

His wife Denise was something else entirely, she was bubbly, chatty and filled the room with energy, she was evolution and worked in creative design. Denise had been prescribed SSRIs 10 years ago, but "they don't help" she sighed. She took a deep breath in "I just have to keep going" and she let go another heavier yearn. I say 'yearn' intentionally because Denise needed help, she couldn't voice it, but she just did. "My recommended treatment is fast, but it would mean that you have to invest a little money on yourselves". They were okay with this, so I explained how they needed to go away for the weekend stay in a swanky hotel, party like they were a couple of teenagers and have passionate sex! I also mentioned that they didn't need to share any of their antics with me next month in our follow up session. Steven's jaw dropped, yet Denise beamed a smile of delight. I then ushered them out of the door as my job was done.

It was almost 6 weeks before the couple returned and what a wonderful surprise. Steven was beaming, he had no recurrence of the pain since our first appointment. Denise's hair style had changed, or so I thought, but it turned out that she had been wearing a wig for the last year. She had been suffering from alopecia (hair loss) and her hair had come out in clumps, not a good look. Since our session, her hair had started to grow back, and she now had the confidence to ditch her wig. "What did you do?" they and you are asking…

The length of time that accompanies a relationship pattern is important to notice. Steven is sameness, 25 years plus before becoming motivated enough to progress a little. Denise was evolution with a chunk of sameness, so when it got to 8 years, she started to crave a little bit of change, it didn't arrive. After two years struggling with lack of motivation, she went to her doctor and the pills were prescribed. The depressive states would come and go, but there was a weight in her chest that just sat there, an ever-present heaviness in her heart.

Steven knew there was something wrong with his wife but didn't know how to help her. So, he did what he thought was right, he worked. Sometimes six or seven days a week, night shifts and extra shifts. He thought making more money would make her happy. When the pain in his legs began, he became more determined to work through it. His subconscious mind could see the signs, the signals his spouse was sending and attempted to reply by preventing him from leaving the house. The pain was not to stop him from walking, it was to encourage him to 'stand up' for their relationship.

By the time the couple had wandered into my office, their goose was cooked. Denise had been metaphorically pulling her hair out, but she didn't know why. Steven was struggling to walk, yet he could cycle to work, strange…! Denise would divorce this year for her own sanity, she acknowledged this by the end of our second and final session. Steven didn't consciously see it coming, but he sensed there was something just not right. Their only child had just turned 18 and it was time for something to change, something, anything!!!

My prescription was 'change', do something crazy, something fun! Now, there they were in my office, laughing and doing just that. They had followed my advice to the letter and had so much fun they'd gone again. They had been making plans, travel, holidays, learning to dance. "But what did you do?" Steven asked, the engineer inside of him needed to know. "You never even mentioned my legs" he said with the innocence of a 4 year old. I smiled at Denise; she knew. Turning back to her husband I talked about how engineering is all about making sure everything is within a certain tolerance, he agreed. "If we try to continue building outside of those tolerances" I continued "stress factors occur". Then, as the happy couple were stepping through the door Steven remarked "How can my legs be okay if you didn't even mention them?" The knowing smile from Denise gave me permission to share, "Steven your physical pain was because you were emotionally crippled" 2 + 2 = 4.

CAN WE EVER REALLY KNOW ANYONE?

We began this chapter with insights drawn from a Simply Red song and I feel it only fitting to close in the same style. *If you don't know me by now* was written by Kenny Gamble and Leon Huff, released by Harold Melvin & The Blue Notes (1972); Simply Red released their cover version in (1989). Gamble and Huff credited the problems they were having in their marriages to the depth of meaning they were able to reach in this song[125].

I hope you, like me, are realising that there are many things to look out for if you are going to share love and happiness in your lifetime. Family Rules sit just over the threshold of the front door, "Come in and make yourself at home!" the host says joyfully, but it would be very naive of you to take him at his word. Have you ever walked into someone's house after being welcomed this way, kicked your shoes off into a corner, your socks in the other, grabbed the TV remote and lay across the sofa? I didn't think so. The offer actually translates to 'there are rules in this house, take care to follow them, however, we won't tell you what they are'. We all know this, yet we play the game.

The song comes from the husband asking his wife to trust him. His job means that he has to work late but when he arrives home *they act like children… argue, fuss and fight*. He acknowledges that he has his own funny moods, yet he is cautious to suggest that his wife might have her own too. This tells us that she

---

[125] https://www.songfacts.com/facts/harold-melvin-the-blue-notes/if-you-dont-know-me-by-now

does and he's just playing the game of not playing the game. The song continues:

'Just get yourself together
Or we might as well say goodbye
What good is a love affair
When you can't see eye to eye'

By the end of the song, we learn that the couple have been together for 20 long years. If we dissect this for a moment, the lines prior to this have asked her to sort herself out. Then we discover he has been having this conversation for two decades and nothing has changed! The song is about Family Rules and as the timescale confirms, nothing has changed since they first got together; they are trapped in 'loyalty'. This has just reminded me of Pauline, who told me how she argued with her husband up until their divorce. Her husband would yell "We have been together for 25 years and you have changed, you are not the girl I married!". Pauline would reply "We're supposed to change! That's the whole point!!"

When we are happy and youthful we dance to the music because it feels good. When we are sad and have the benefit of experience (older) we learn the lyrics. I can't help but feel if the songwriters had known more about Family Rules and their subconscious motivational patterns, their relationship troubles could have been sorted long ago. This would, however, have impacted a beautiful song. I encourage you to find the Family Rules within other songs too.

CHAPTER SUMMARY

We discovered Relationships have subconscious filters and time plays a motivational factor within them.

Sameness	Sameness with Evolution	Evolution	Evolution with Difference	Difference
		Time in Years		
25	15	7-5	3-2	1.5-1

He who plays the fool may be smarter than he who thinks the fool is a fool.

Funny Logical (Phonological) Ambiguities can deliver different meanings (ewe sea) and different meanings can help to shift a person's reality.

The Sameness relationship filter when in a No/My environment can create a sameness Your/.

The 'chemical imbalance' of the brain is a myth and has no evidence to support it.

Loyalty does not mean loving or passionate, it can mean they are just turning up every day!

If we mistake loyalty for love we may end up demotivated and there can be psychophysiological pushback, as the mind sends out an SOS!

I like Simply Red and songs with Family Rules tucked inside of them.

7

LOYALTY ABOVE ALL ELSE

*"Some people aren't loyal to you; they
are loyal to their need of you. Once their
needs change, so does their loyalty."*
Unknown

This next Family Rule can run in a marriage or a long-term commitment to the wrong person. It's great if your patterns match but if they don't this can prove to be unhealthy for both sides as the Ahluwalia and Challen family know only too well. Although we have been discussing compliance and obedience throughout the book, you may be surprised that 'Loyalty' is a Family Rule that sits best with the sameness pattern. People with this rule may have a stoical, indifferent, long-suffering, bond/bind with their partner.

As Tina Turner put it, "What's Love got to do with it?" Loyalty can take a relationship way past its best by date. When the phrase 'I love you' is uttered like Tourette's, with no passion or intimacy, then these three little words that so many of us long to hear, just become a sound.

Trapped inside a codependent* relationship where the dysfunctional childhood of a person continues to impinge on their adult life, the day-to-day routine becomes one of rinse and repeat. Look up Adverse Childhood Experiences (ACEs), which we covered earlier. Some can develop codependency without ACEs, however, as we have demonstrated, if a person feels their life is threatened by a No/My they can become codependant (Your/.) within a couple of days. Their craving for routine and sameness becomes logical as it costs less energy. A No/My however, needs to keep the blame game running to ensure that their codependent partner doesn't have the time or the inclination to awaken from plight.

*The American Psychological Association define Codependency:

1. the state of being mutually reliant, for example, a relationship between two individuals who are emotionally dependent on one another.
2. a dysfunctional relationship pattern in which an individual is psychologically dependent on (or controlled by) a person who has a pathological addiction (e.g., alcohol, gambling). —**codependent** *adj.*

Let's be clear, caring for a person who is needy doesn't mean that you are codependent. However, it can become codependency if you are desperately trying to get some kind of recognition or reward. The compulsion to serve can be born out of a Family Rule that revolves around 'loyalty'. I wrote the short story *What if Love were Jellybeans in a Jar?*,[126] to show how easily a person can fall into the clutches of this very real human condition.

You may be very surprised to learn what codependency is and how easily you can become trapped in its clutches. The 'jellybeans' metaphor I have used over the years in workshops

---

[126] https://www.amazon.co.uk/What-Love-were-Jelly-Beans/dp/1984258842

and one to one client work, it strikes a chord with those who are imprisoned inside it. The crazy thing is no one has ever booked a session to overcome codependency. If you are inside the trap, then the Family Rule is 'tell no one', so you will appear with chronic pain or a chronic dis-ease that prevents you from being YOU.

Your dis-ease (uneasy with your situation) may increase tenfold as you struggle to cope with or adapt to the changes in your life or certain aspects of it. Hans Selye believed that our failure to adapt was the cause of our disease. R.D. Laing tells us that psychiatrist Theodore Lidz saw "schizophrenia as a failure of human adaptation"[127]. Laing proposed an 'objective' view of schizophrenia as "a label affixed by some people to others in situations where an interpersonal disjunction of a particular kind is occurring" (ibid. p57). If we were to look out at the world around us today, where poverty continues to spread, misinformation increases, fears for our health, safety and future intensify, perhaps we are all failing to adapt to the homogenised 21st century existence. What if psychophysiological dis-ease is our spirit, the 'You' and the 'Me' kicking back at the unnatural cage that our masters have built around us!

If we see dis-ease as an SOS signal that our mind is projecting out into the universe; then our next problem is, what if the cavalry arrives? Trapped inside a Your/. motivation we must be loyal to our master, who will remain unblemished, and our relationship will continue to sail, long after it should have sunk! The No/my is trapped within a codependent relationship with the Your/. If the Your/. stops complying, the power and influence of the No/My stops too.

---

[127] http://www.willhall.net/files/RDLaingPoliticsOfExperienceAnd-BirdOfParadise.pdf

KARPMAN'S DRAMA TRIANGLE

This chapter wouldn't be complete without the introduction of Steve Karpman's Drama Triangle[128]. The Drama Triangle was built on the work of Canadian born, American psychiatrist Eric Berne[129]. Berne developed Transactional Analyses (TA). TA as a psychological theory looks at interactions or 'transactions' that an individual uses between another or others. These transactions are then analysed to reach greater understanding for the speaker and to reflect what message may be received by the listener.

Berne's international best-selling book *The Games People Play* [130] highlights the many interactions and transactions that are used in dysfunctional relationships. Berne defined 'the games' as:

"A game is an ongoing series of complementary ulterior transactions progressing to a well-defined, predictable outcome. Descriptively, it is a recurring set of transactions… with a concealed motivation… or gimmick."

Karpman believed the Parent-Adult-Child positions were acted out as victim-rescuer-persecutor. You may know some people who are seriously addicted to drama. You could drop them anywhere on the planet and within an hour they will have found something or someone with which to create a drama. Whether in the home, the office or even government, the Drama Triangle can give clear insight to the codependent, contemptuous actions that negatively impact families and groups, great or small.

The triangle is made up of the Victim-Rescuer-Persecutor. If you observe someone playing the drama game, you can

---

[128] https://karpmandramatriangle.com/
[129] https://ericberne.com/transactional-analysis/
[130] https://ericberne.com/games-people-play/

become dizzy watching them ping from one position to the other.

The Persecutor: Angry, aggressive passively and openly, bullying and very demanding.

The Rescuer: Fails to see that people can look after themselves. Self-sacrificing, overwhelming, needs to be needed.

The Victim: Poor me. Blame others, moan, and complain, helpless, needy, manipulative.

The origin of the unconscious driver behind a person wanting or needing to play the victim role can be found in Family Rules. As a child were you taught by your parents to lie or to tell the truth? I'm sure we would all assign to the latter, however if your parents got angry and yelled "Did you do it!" you would learn to be afraid to tell the truth, fearing the unknown consequences of their obvious rage. The tonality and non-verbal communication that accompanies the message suggest a known punishment to the subconscious mind, which at a young age chooses the lie as the path of least resistance. If your parents were curious and kind, creating learning experiences, where feedback was given and received then you will have grown, being able to trust and to know it's value. There are many for whom this was not the case, and they find denial more comfortable than speaking the truth.

From the first lie, the first move away from the safety of our carer, we step into individual selfhood. We adopt a primitive survival response, which can then be used to project responsibility onto others instead of having to own up and be accountable for our own actions. So long as we have someone or something else to blame then our mind seems to believe that this is okay, which would support why many people are driven to victimhood.

Karpman's original model had only these three positions, I adapted the image below to clearly show a way out of the game. The player/s enter the game by seeing the source of their problems as external. The more they try, the more they fail. They all seek to be acknowledged; the act of seeking maintains their outward focus. One could argue they seek attention as even when they gain acknowledgement it's still not enough. The key is to turn ones attention inwardly. When we focus on how we are feeling and set boundaries for our own personal needs, then we can transcend the game. The 'C' can then be for centred or congruent, where you can sit and notice the others around you, as they play the game of not playing the game.

How to Leave the Game

From a position in the centre of the triangle the key is to remain congruent, calm, curious and open. As you become more accustomed to this position the other players will back away. If they offer you onto the game with a "Why have you done this" or "Why didn't you do that?" simply smile from the inside out and say, "That's interesting". 'That's interesting' is a neutral statement that keeps you centred. When they attempt to provoke you with "Why is it interesting?" Shine from the inside out and reply, "It's just interesting". If you say, "because blah, blah, blah" then you have stepped onto the triangle.

Stay away from asking yourself 'Why?' it only causes a spin of emotions. Instead, ask what is motivating me to act the way that I do? Am I attempting to manipulate the situation so that I gain or am I genuinely wanting to help others? Do I have an expectation? If we need something in return for helping others, then our actions are dysfunctional, there is a Family Rule in operation. Just keep practicing and developing, we are all learners.

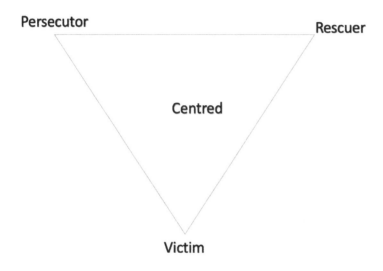

You will know when you are out of the Drama Triangle when:

You are assertive not persecuting

You can accept your vulnerability without being a victim

You can care without needing to be a Carer.

To care or caring is something that you do, it's a behaviour or an action, whereas a Carer is an identity, it's who you are.

HAPPY FAMILIES-THE HOUSE OF CARDS

Helen presented with chronic fatigue, which was the best way that she could describe her condition to me. Over a period of ill health spanning two decades, she had suffered many symptoms and had been diagnosed by various doctors (including neurologists and cardiologists) as having ME/ CFS, fibromyalgia, chronic vestibular migraine, rheumatoid arthritis and postural orthostatic tachycardia syndrome (PoTS), Trigeminal neuralgia (TN or TGN) to name but a few. Any one of these conditions is bad, but when you have all of them, you get the idea that the symptoms may be universal. At the very least they are very difficult to separate or specifically define. Each clinician she visited was able to view her symptoms from their own specialism, so she had many names to identify her problem, but no handle to take hold of. Each new clinic she attended filled her with hope, they did lots of tests and eventually told her that she would just have to learn to live with it..! Helen settled for the term 'Chronic fatigue' using it as an umbrella statement, with which she and whoever she was talking to, could get a general idea of what was going on for her.

By the time Helen was 28 she had been married and divorced twice, had three children, seven miscarriages, a hip replacement owing to chronic pain and the erosion of her hip joint. You and I both know there is something really significant and scary sitting inside the mind of this lady, but what?

Helen openly revealed that she had been unable to keep any steady relationships with men, she always chose the 'wrong ones'. Her parents never liked any of them and her male partners were of a similar opinion reference her parents. All she ever wanted was Prince Charming to come and rescue her, but she never knew why she felt the urge to be rescued. Most of her childhood memories and even parts of her adult life were hazy, she was often bedridden for months at a time. It was during one of her better days that 'it' happened.

Gillian (Helen's mother) had popped round for tea, the kids were now in bed, and she was washing up in the kitchen. "He's a pig, like the rest of them," Gillian muttered as she dried the cup in her hand, twisting the tea-towel tightly into the defenceless mug. "Who?" Helen tentatively enquired. "Who do you think?" came the reply. Helen shrugged. "Your father!" Gillian barked. Helen was dumbfounded, never in her life had she heard her mother speak ill of her husband, her father, her dad. "How do you mean?" Helen probed for more details. Her mother stared at her with a blank expressionless face, she had something to say, something to share with her daughter, her little girl. Gillian blinked and came back from the trance she had just stepped into, "Nothing! It's nothing" she asserted whilst coming back online. Gillian put on her coat "Just forget it!" she said, as the front door closed behind her. 2 + 2 = 5.

"I'd never seen her like this, ever," Helen continued. There was too much in the "nothing" for there to be nothing, but what was it? Helen was an only child; her mother had miscarried seven times in total; three before she fell pregnant with her and then four times after her birth. She stopped trying for another by the time Helen was five. I mention this because, this is the order in which the information was presented to me. Helen was feeding me breadcrumbs, hoping that I would follow her trail, which I did. Just like the Hansel and Gretel story, I felt a foreboding in the nothing ahead of us.

"I woke up from a thought, a dream, a nightmare!" Helen explained. She was physically shaking; her body and mind were entering an abreaction; she was reliving the exact state that she had been in on that night. Her mother had momentarily broken the Family Rule, one glitch in the informational fabric of their shared reality. The years of haze and darkness cleared and scene after scene flowed onto the screen inside her mind. She understood why her mother stopped trying for a baby, she understood, why she had been ill for so long, she realised why she couldn't maintain a relationship or find a 'good man' a good man like her father! From the age of four her father had begun to abuse her and this continued until she was 22 years old. Helen had been in a steady relationship with Graeme for the past three years and she was getting herself into a good place. Her dad hated Graeme and despised the fact that she was settling, now it was becoming clearer…

I know what you are thinking…How on earth can a 22-year-old still be having sex with her father and not report it? Family Rules! Welcome to the world of trauma. Research has shown that if sexual abuse happens in early childhood there is very little chance of the victim consciously remembering the experience, however there is every chance that the body will keep the score[131]. There is evidence suggesting that approximately 40% of people who have experienced sexual abuse and or extreme violence can have total amnesia and approximately 60% experience partial amnesia[132]. Professor Mark Johnson and I explore this further in our current paper, which has just been published[133]. For now, let me assure you Helen had zero conscious knowledge of what her father had been doing 'to her', until the Family Rule had been broken. Please note 'to her' and not 'with her' even though Helen was over the age of sexual consent, she was not a consciously willing subject.

Remember: given the right conditions good people will do bad things. Each time the conditions were right for her father, he acted on it, reducing his daughter to a sexual object. It would be like he had given her 'Flunitrazepam' a central nervous system depressant. It is similar to diazepam but approximately 10 times more potent. It is a tasteless, odourless tablet that can be crushed and dissolved in liquid. It's more widely known as Rohypnol the date rape drug. The difference between what was happening to Helen and those who had been raped with Rohypnol was consciousness. Rohypnol victims have no conscious memory of the act as they are invariably unconscious, but they do have an awareness afterwards that something has happened and usually call the police. This was not the same for Helen who was conscious and actively took part. Unlike others who had been drugged however, she would not awaken from the trance her father had induced.

---

[131] van der Kolk, B.A., and J.W. Hopper. 2001. Exploring the nature of traumatic memory: combining clinical knowledge with laboratory methods. *Journal of Aggression, Maltreatment & trauma* 4: 9-31

[132] IVSEA https://www.memoiretraumatique.org/campagnes-et-colloques/2015-campagne-stop-au-deni.html

[133] Hudson M, Johnson MI. Definition and Attributes of the Emotional Memory Images underlying Psychophysiological Dis-ease. Frontiers in Psychology https://doi.org/10.3389/fpsyg.2022.947952

Even as I write this I can still see the 4-year-old girl in the face of this almost 34-year-old female. Her bouts of fatigue, her varying health symptoms were brought on to keep her from visiting her daddy. All this time, all this illness, Helen reconciled, her mind was trying to protect her... 2 + 2 = 4.

In a similar way Helen's life could be likened to the tip of the tongue effect. When you've bumped into someone, what's his name? It drives you mad all day long, what's his name? Then at 2.30 am you wake up and his name is there for you. That tiny break in the Family Rule set her mind on finding everything to do with 'the nothing' her mother had emphasised. Our new paper suggests that an emotional memory image acts like a mental tag inside the mind of the victim. It won't go away, it can't go away, but every time Helen was alone with her father, she would fall into the original state of mind, and he would physically rape her. Our victim never knew she was a victim, until now. The deletion filter was gone, and tons of graphic data were now flooding her mind. How could she not have raised the alarm, especially at 22 years old? In those moments Helen's mind went into autopilot and she did what she had always done! When her mother broke the Family Rule of 'Happy Family' Helen gained conscious access to everything that had previously sat outside of her mental map.

I mention Helen and this particular Family Rule because there are many people who continue to have their rights violated or suffer trauma at the hands of No/My's. These authority figures who have no rules for themselves and inflict appalling rules on others are no longer hidden from us, they are being called out (see[134] [135]). The challenge for the masses within our

---

[134] Fauci Book Robert F Kennedy Junior
[135] Peter R. Breggin Psychiatrists Peter R. Breggin and his wife Ginger COVID-19 and the Global Predators: We Are the Prey

global family becomes even greater as we are herded, divided, and isolated by an ever more totalitarian rule.

With each 'political parent' that is identified as an abuser (No/My), our physical and mental wellbeing is punished as we struggle to consciously grasp that they do not care about what happens to us, their children. "They must care" the voice inside my mind demands, I feel afraid as I write this, my heart swells and saltwater wells in my eyes. The reality of our parents not caring for us, wanting us to die, to starve and to freeze as the winter of 2022 approaches is a hard-hitting fact. The scent of the Your/. mentality fills the air as the Dutch M.D. and psychoanalyst Joost A.M. Meerloo (1903-1976) articulated in his book The Rape of The Mind.[136]

> "Totalitarianism is man's escape from the fearful realities
> of life into the virtual womb of the leaders. The individual's
> actions are directed from this womb – from the inner sanctum
> man need no longer assume responsibility for his own life.
> The order and logic of the prenatal world reign. There is peace
> and silence, the peace of utter submission." (ibid., 129).

If we observe the words above from a Family Rules position, 'totalitarianism' and the 'virtual womb' are created as a safe haven. This "safety" is offered by the very parents/leaders that have perpetuated the false narratives through the media, leaving the children/us craving some stability. To better understand 'prenatal world reign', imagine existing on a planet where you are without the experience of the real world, living your life as a tiny cog, void of imagination, connection, or love, (life inside Plato's Cave). History informs us the 'peace of utter

---

[136] The Rape of the Mind: The Psychology of Thought Control, Menti-cide, and Brainwashing Paperback – 25 Feb. 2015

submission' is a miserable existence, the complete Your/. a substandard life of serfdom.

As we have explored throughout this book, poor mental and physical health accompany this tragic loss of spirituality, of self-ownership. We are informed there are many people who are afraid of living and being responsible for themselves, but what if they have been lied to? Perhaps, like the elephant, the masses were enslaved in early childhood, so soon in their development that they would know no other. A worrying thought indeed for those who were raised by a digital baby-sitter (T.V. or other digital device, which operates as the wall in Plato's cave to influence your development).

Meerloo made a study of how the state was able to apply systematic mental pressure on its people to create a submissive population (Your/.). Once in this mindset the totalitarian (No/My) can imprint whatever 'truth' they desire onto the minds of their victims. There is peace at the end for all those who follow and maintain the No/My rules, 'the peace of utter submission'. This 'peace' we've covered in earlier chapters eroding love, connection, spirituality and replacing it with a mechanistic realm, void of compassion or humanity.

I remember taking the boys on a certain ride in Disneyland, it seemed harmless enough on the surface, but its message sent a chill down my spine, and still does. The ride is called 'It's a small world after all' and it takes you around the planet from nation to nation, where despite the differences in each population, they all sang 'It's a small world after all' over and over again. I was reminded of the automata that the French philosopher René Descartes was reputedly fond of.[137]

---

[137] https://www.nature.com/articles/d41586-018-05773y#:~:text=The%20French%20philosopher%20Ren%C3%A9%20Descartes,the%20philosopher's%20death%20in%201650.

There is an unverified myth which tells of Descartes creating a walking talking simulacrum of his daughter Francine, who died tragically at the age of 5 from scarlet fever. Descartes can be seen then as a father who loved his daughter so much that he was unable to let her go. In Mary Shelly's book, Dr Victor Frankenstein grappled with the ability to bypass the pain of bereavement when he created the 'monster', a creature without a soul. The story begins with a passionate doctor who, as his ambition grows, sees his moral compass deplete, obsessed as "his science becomes more sinister and misdirected[138]". Shelly invites us to view the creature as an alienated soulless organism, created by a mechanistic science who needs our pity. The creature is given life, but what sort of life? Without family, without compassion, without humanity, surely it's the fragility of human life that makes it so worthwhile, to live, to love, to die. Perhaps, the No/My's do not fear death because they, like Frankenstein's monster, are soulless and devoid of compassion, loving only things, objects, and possessions.

The mechanistic future under totalitarian (No/My) leadership is not as short lived, I propose, as many historians make out. Remember Sally Challen? She survived as a Your/. for 40 years and only broke free owing to an overwhelming change in her circumstances. How much further are we the people prepared to bend? First we clap for the NHS, then we bend the knee to support the latest narrative, what next? Sacrificing our children at the Covid alter or freezing the vulnerable to death with overinflated energy prices..! (Oops! I stepped on my soapbox again). Let's take a look at another set of below conscious drivers, to help make a little more sense out of the Family Rules within this particular chapter.

---

[138] https://www.nature.com/articles/535490a

POWER, ACHIEVEMENT OR AFFILIATION?

In the 1960s American psychologist and Harvard Professor, David McClelland developed a theory of needs, also known as Achievement Theory of Motivation[139]. His work categorises human motivation into 3 main areas, Power, Achievement or Affiliation. Although we all share these needs, in certain individuals one of them can be more dominant than others. He then goes on to explain what and how needs are met and how they have to be approached.

The beauty of McClelland's theory is it is applicable regardless of our age, sex, race, or culture. We all possess these needs at varying levels, given the right context the main driver can take over. These particular traits fit within Family Rules as McClelland affirmed the specific needs of an individual can be acquired, shaped, and influenced via their life experiences, over time.

The three needs of Power, Achievement and Affiliation can significantly impact a person's behaviour, regardless of their demography, culture, or wealth. These motivational traits are driven by real-life experiences and the views from within our mental maps. Let's take a closer look at what these traits look like in the real world.

Need for Power

The need for power is the main driver within a person to hold control and authority over another. They also influence/change their decision in accordance with his own needs or desires. The need to enhance their self-esteem and reputation drives these people. They desire their views and ideas to be

---

[139] McClelland, D. C., & McClelland, D. C. (1961). *Achieving society* (Vol. 92051). Simon and Schuster.

accepted/implemented over the views and ideas of others. These people are strong leaders, they can be best suited to influential positions. They either belong to Personal or Institutional power motivator groups. If they are a personal power motivator they would have the need to control others, an institutional power motivator seeks to lead and coordinate a team towards an end.

The individuals motivated by the need for power have a desire to control and influence others. Competition motivates them and they like to win an argument. Status and recognition are something they aspire to; they do not like to be on the losing side. They are self-disciplined and expect the same from their peers and teams. They do not mind playing a zero-sum game, where, for one person to win, another must lose, and collaboration is not an option. This motivational type is accompanied by needs for personal prestige, and better personal status.

Having said all of the above, there are still plenty of people who can wield their power for the benefit of others, but it's not their preferred driver. When we reach the last straw, when enough is enough, SNAP! The power from within us is unleashed, as we discovered with Kiranjit Ahluwalia, Sally Challen and the countless others, who for their own reasons, decided to rise against the wrongdoer.

Need for Power: Require influence and are competitive.
Typical behaviours:
High Power - Demands blind loyalty and harmony,
does not tolerate disagreement.
Low Power - Remains aloof, maintains social distance.

POWER

Need for Achievement

A person who is driven by the need for achievement will be continually driven to do better, just for the sake of doing it. This person loves a challenge and wants to be in charge of their own success. Imagine growing up in a family where your mother or father need to be the best mother or father? It sounds like a recipe for disaster, as life is definitely not a game of perfection. Hypocrisy may spread into the mind of your child, who attempts to fit into your false reality, only to fail. Eating disorders, body dysmorphia and psychophysiological dis-ease can develop within these children. Their mind attempts to be someone that they cannot be, wanting to be seen by a parent who is blinded to any imperfections within their perfect family.

Achievement-oriented individuals will change the situation or the location if they feel like it is not meeting their needs. They do not like working in groups because they do not like having limited control over the outcome. Instead, they prefer to do work where the results are clear and visible. As I wrote these last lines I heard a large penny drop inside my mind. I've only just realised that I am a highly motivated by achievement, it's an itch that drives me. As I rationalise this in my head, I remember that my grandmother told my mother and her 6 siblings their father had left them to play professional football for Leeds United. I was 50 years old when, after creating a family tree, I discovered that my grandfather had been killed in action at the start of World War II. My parents never knew. The lie that my grandmother told was to save her children from the grief of losing their father, but it created a schism in the family. Like a fracture in the universe, that has been passed down for me and me alone to heal. A tear in the essence of my soul, a tear that has welled in this realisation.

Just before my 50th birthday I left my marriage, without any real knowledge of 'why' and now, out of all the infinite possibilities, I find the answer in the quiet of this room as I write. My need to achieve drove me out of the world I had known for over 25 years into the nothing, where I could create something new. My achievement filter prevented me from sharing the load, the burden of paying the bills and creating a living was all on my shoulders, because I failed to share it.

ACHIEVEMENT

Need for Achievement: Takes personal responsibility, needs feedback, takes moderate risks
Typical behaviours:
High achievers - Must win at any cost, must be on top, and receive credit.
Low achievers - Fears failure, avoids responsibility.

Need for Affiliation

If the need for affiliation is a person's main driver, they will be essentially motivated to have interpersonal and social connections. They seek to work in groups by creating friendly and lasting relationships. Instead of competing, they lean towards collaboration with others and usually avoids high-risk situations and uncertainty. Their strongest desire is to be loved and accepted within the group; they need to be needed; you might see them as 'people pleasers'. They have a huge fear of rejection, which drives their need to conform and play life by the rule book. Whatever the social norms of the group, they will follow in order to avoid rejection. They are risk averse, always seeking the safer way to do things, afraid of being caught outside of the group. They place a high value on their relationships, this can mean that they will stay at the same job for years even after they should have had many pay increases and improved working conditions. If they don't have children of their own, they will be 'Auntie' or 'Uncle' to others as they are very caring by nature, seeking to continually add to their connections. The biggest challenge this particular person will have is progression; they are simply not motivated to do better and are content to stay in the same position.

Hopefully this particular trait can help you to understand that friend of yours who is in a hopeless relationship, unloved and unappreciated, yet he/she still stays, no matter what. The thought of leaving the relationship and disappointing others creates greater pain than the misery of remaining and putting up with a daily tirade of verbal/mental abuse. If you attempt to point any of this out to them, they will make excuses for their partners and a huge deletion filter automatically covers any of the wrongdoings. They are prime candidates for surviving within a hypocritical environment where a No/My rules, they are more likely to conform and become a Your/..

If, however, you are already in this pattern then your deletion filter will just erase this information from your mind, you can continue with your glass of wine, or whatever 'fix' you need in order to ease your suffering. Tragically, this pattern will never come into the therapy room for relationship matters, but they may appear with chronic fatigue, chronic pain or an unexplainable psychophysiological disorder. If you are the therapist or coach on this occasion, remember they are playing the game of not playing the game, if you point this out to them, you will be punished! The client may complain about you to a higher authority, or they may just not contact you again. This is why you have to be sneaky when dealing with Family Rules, if you don't hit the target first time, there may never be a next.

AFFILIATION

Need for Affiliation: Require acceptance and friendship, they are cooperative.
Typical behaviours:
High Affiliation - Desires control of everyone and everything, exaggerates own position and resources.
Low Affiliation - Dependent/ subordinate, minimizes own position and resources.

As we can see the need for Power, Achievement and Affiliation resides in all of us to greater or lesser degrees. Depending on the context, the key is to apply these to our parents and to figure out where that affects us and our other relationships.

When Power meets Power

When James eventually came to see me for an appointment, I'd heard via the therapists grapevine that he was unreachable, yet he was going from therapist to therapist in search of help. He clearly wanted someone to reach him, didn't he?

James had been depressed for over 20 years owing to the shape of his nose and 2 years prior to our session, James had undergone plastic surgery to correct his problem. He had never been happy with his nose as it was and he was sure that surgery was the answer, it wasn't! James complained that the operation was an utter failure, and he underwent a second procedure, which he still wasn't happy with (you don't say). James then fell into a deeper depression as his nose was now "totally ruined" he explained. He had before and after photographs to show me and I have to be honest, I couldn't tell the difference in any of them, but I wasn't the guy with body dysmorphia.

In his mid to late 40s, dressed in a grey suite with a shirt and a crucifix dangling over the top of his tie, the answer to his problem suddenly struck me. "You're a Catholic?" I asked, "Roman Catholic!" he barked. "You're a liar" I chipped back. James glared at me and then asserted "I've heard that you are unorthodox in your approach, but I will leave if you continue down this line of conversation". Never being one to stop in the middle of a double bind I questioned "Hmmm…you're a blasphemer then..?" "That's it! I'm out of here!!" James was on his feet and heading to the door. "You're the one that isn't happy being made in God's own image, not me" I confidently declared. James froze with his back to me and a hand on the door handle. He slowly turned to face me, the rage had gone, replaced by confusion and the beginnings of a grin, a big cheesy grin, "You bugger!" he laughed. "Would you like a cup of tea, now?" I chuckled.

Thanks to my knowledge of Family Rules and a tiny insight of Christianity, I was able to discern a leverage point where I could shift James's attention. James had an anger inside of him sitting under the surface, ready to blow at any point with anyone. His auditory tone as he spoke to me, inflected downwards, gave the clue that he was Power motivated. This being the case I would need to increase my influence to a higher Power than his. God, given the crucifix and Roman Catholic, was the logical choice. Provoking him would ensure that he was in the exact state of mind which was causing his problem. This is what I call a 'waking trance' or a 'living trance' as it is present whilst the client is going about their everyday life. The point at which James has his hand on the door is also his maximum flight response, he's paid for an hour yet he is running away with 45 minutes left on the clock; why?

James was physically larger than me and he was packed with rage, but instead of choosing to fight, he opted for flight. The problem with this survival response is James never gets to evolve to the next level, he remains aggressive but never assertive, which are completely different states of mind. As I verbalise the Family Rule the trance is broken, James is elevated from the primitive flight stress response and his smart brain is able to bring consciousness into the moment – split-second unlearning. It's also important to note I paced, matched and then led my client Power v Power, up until his strategy failed him and then Affiliation v Affiliation as we both laughed together. To the untrained eye, one might think me a callous uncaring and unknowledgeable individual, but there is madness in my method and method in my madness.

CHAPTER SUMMARY

We discovered that 'loyalty' may not be such a wonderful trait to have as it can cause us to remain in the wrong environments for far too long.

Codependency is a hugely unhealthy way to live one's life, it's needed when we are children but then it should lead to independence and eventually interdependence as we grow and flourish together.

The Karpman Drama Triangle and how to step off the game. No longer trapped between Rescuer, Persecutor or Victim.

Victimhood is derived from the first lie.

"That's interesting" will keep you out of the game.

Whole chunks of time can be shrouded in amnesia until the Family Rule is broken and then the unknown becomes the known. The tragedy is the person also discovers that they have always known.

Totalitarianism = Hypocrisy = No/My

No/My need Your/. and vice versa
Power, Achievement or Affiliation are the 3 main subconscious drivers we all have them and some of us are influenced more than others in certain contexts.

Power or Achievement can become No/My
Affiliation is more likely to become Your/.

8
A COLLECTION OF FAMILY RULES

*"Primitive societies live by the Rule of
Might, and the strong prevail. Advanced
societies live by the Rule of Law, and the
privileged prevail. Enlightened societies live
by the Rule of Love, and
everyone is lifted higher."*
Mike Dooley

Virginia Satir's work encourages us to become excited about ourselves. When you think about it, you and I are the only ones of 'us' in the entire universe[140] we are pretty special. Hopefully this book is delivering you new insights, with which you can discover greater opportunities to rise and shine. As Canadian author Marianne Williamson reminds us "It is our light, not our darkness that most frightens us"[141]. It's with this lightness of spirit that we wander into our final chapter, where we will discover some of the many Family Rules that act as gatekeepers, preventing us from living our best life.

---

[140] Satir VM. *New Peoplemaking*. 2nd ed. Science and Behavior Books; 1989.
[141] Williamson M. (1992). *A return to love: reflections on the principles of a course in miracles* (1st ed.). HarperCollins.

In Chapter 4 of The Saboteur Within[142], I look at 'The circle of life' and where in particular you find yourself spending the most time or energy. 'Energy' and 'time' are the essence of our life on earth and who knows how far that life extends when we consider the metaphysical universe? All I know is the vast majority of people are either low on energy, never have enough time or both. Hopefully as you unhook from your Family Rules you will regain your energy and mastery of time, instead of having it control you.

In the diagram below you can see a pie chart divided into 8 sections: Physical Environment; Money; Body and Health; Friends and Family; Romance; Spiritual and Personal Growth; Recreation and Creativity; Career. Over the past 10 years or so, I've created a list, not an exhaustive list I might add, but just enough for you to get a feel for how Family Rules may be impacting you in a certain context. I used to offer the circle to clients so they could go away and complete it as part of their development. They would change the titles to best fit their context. For example: some may see 'Money' and 'Career' as the same thing so they combined the two and created 'Wealth', then others would see 'Wealth' as being connected to 'Spiritual' and 'Physical', so there is no cast iron rule here, just see how you go. The challenge is of course finding your own Family Rule as it will sit outside of your conscious awareness, so maybe you can work through this particular chapter with a friend?

[142] Hudson M. The Saboteur within: The Definitive Guide to Overcoming Self Sabotage. Createspace Independent Publishing Platform; 2011.

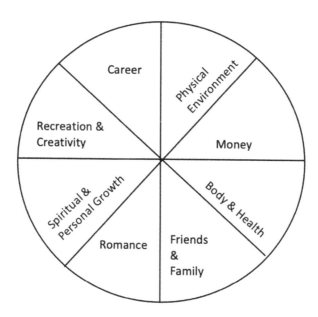

RULES, RULES, RULES

- You can't burn the candle at both ends
- Don't push me
- Don't fidget
- Three score years and ten, that'll do me
- Life begins at forty
- You'll always have your looks
- You must kiss your aunt/relatives
- If you miss school because you're ill, you can't go out to play
- You've got to toughen up
- Always tell the truth

- A woman's work is never done
- There's no need to look good
- The house must be spotless for guests
- That's a boy's thing
- Grown-ups are always right
- It's different for girls
- The Policeman will take you away
- People don't practice what they preach
- It is important to create beauty and warmth in a home
- A woman makes the home
- If a job's worth doing, it's worth doing right

- It's not what you do. It's how you do it
- Two wrongs don't make a right
- Great minds think alike
- Knowledge is supreme
- Professionals do well anywhere
- If your IQ is low, you're useless
- You are your own boss
- Education and knowledge always rule
- Religion always creates conflict
- Science subjects are more important than others
- You're stupid
- You'll never go to college
- I could've told you that
- Girls are smarter than boys
- You'll never finish that
- Always stick to what you know
- You must always love your parents
- Your mother/father is always right
- Always obey your parents
- You've let me down
- You're too big/small to do that
- You're too big for your boots
- Tell one lie and you will need to tell ten
- You are who you are – you can't change it
- Always respect your elders
- Don't hang your dirty washing out in public
- What's said in here stays in here
- You weren't born in a field
- You'll never set the world right
- Your friends bring you down
- It's no good asking me
- Where there's a will, there's a way
- Never judge a book by its cover
- Youth is wasted on the young
- You'll be the death of me
- Do you think I'm made of money
- I want never gets
- Money doesn't grow on trees
- Don't answer back
- Never talk to strangers
- Neither a borrower or a lender be
- If you do that the bogey man will get you
- Don't answer back
- Visitors are more important than family members
- You are what you eat

- Clean your plate, there's children starving in Africa
- You'll sit there until you're finished
- It's just puppy fat
- You'll get what you're given and be grateful for it
- Never trust a man who doesn't drink
- You have to obey the rules even if they make you ill
- Food and meal times create tension
- You must have three meals a day
- They'll eat when they're hungry
- You'll eat anything if you are hungry enough
- You can't leave the table until everyone is finished
- You're ungrateful
- You're too fat to run
- I'm hungry and I'm angry
- What's for tea? A walk around the table until you're fed up!
- Don't eat between meals
- Never waste anything
- Be seen and not heard
- Father's music is more important
- Classical music is most important
- Popular music is fun

- Don't shout
- Eat with your mouth closed
- Never tell lies
- Do as you are told
- People are people – everyone is valuable
- Never take no for an answer
- You are who you are – you can't change it
- It doesn't matter
- You must do this because…no explanation
- You must do as I say
- I'm going to put you in a home
- Asking for help is a sign of failure
- You made your own bed now lie in it!
- Act your age not your shoe size
- It's better to give than to receive
- Enough is enough. Wait till you father/mother gets home
- It's weak to have emotions
- Don't cry in public
- Don't express your emotions
- Crying is a sign of weakness
- Don't be over emotional, it's too sentimental

- Showing affection creates tension
- Women who express feelings are lesser human beings
- I am responsible for my mother's happiness
- Expressing feelings can be painful
- What goes around comes around
- Pride comes before a fall
- Cleanliness is next to Godliness
- God helps those who help themselves
- Better the devil you know
- God and spirituality are a load of nonsense
- God is punishing and to be feared
- If you're good you'll go to heaven

I'm sure that you can add some rules of your own here, there are some which may seem ridiculous to you and that's because it's not from your family. Let's take a look at a relatively simple Family Rule 'You must always love your parents'. On the surface this seems simple enough, right? Now, let's take a look at how this overarching rule may impact other areas of our lives. For example, "If you love me then you should know what makes me happy". If this is said to you by your mother or father, who you must love without question, Houston we have a problem! The implications of attempting to make sense of this Family Rule can lead you a not so merry dance. Let's break it down:

"If you love me then you should know what makes me happy"

If you love me – this already creates doubt, of course I love you mummy, but do you love me? Have I upset you? Is that why you're using the word if? Do I really love you? Mummy do you know that I don't really love you and that's why you're using 'if'? Am I going to die! These are just examples of the kind of crazy questions that set off inside your mind, whenever a Family Rule is activated. The amount of time and energy that could be spent attempting to resolve this unresolvable statement is unquantifiable. The '*Am I going to die!*' is added as all roads lead to survival and the greatest odds for achieving it.

If you love me then – Implied causation. Whatever follows the 'then' I must obey because I love you mummy. If this, then that. If I don't obey then that will mean that I don't love you, so I must obey. Otherwise, you will see that I don't love you and then you might stop loving me. Then I will die.

You should know what makes me happy – Only I know what makes mummy happy, not daddy, not anyone else just me. Mummy isn't happy and it's my fault because I don't know why she is not happy, but I should know because I love my mummy. If I don't know what makes mummy happy then I mustn't love her, but I do love her, maybe she will stop loving me if I can't make her happy. Then I will die!

I hope you have figured out why Theodore Lidz and R.D. Laing dedicated so much time to schizophrenia, seemingly simple statements can take up lots of headspace. Both eminent psychiatrists realised that no amount of medication would or could undo the knot inside the mind, created by *Folie en Famille*, Family Rules.

One particular client springs to mind as I write this. Elizabeth, a lady in her late 50s, who was referred to me by her GP, he described her as having "alcohol problems". Elizabeth and Lez, her husband of 35 years, had just sold their company for several million pounds and they should have been set for a very happy and early retirement. The only problem was Lez had found love in another woman and had moved on to another relationship. Elizabeth knew all about it, but she simply would not let her husband have an amicable divorce. This is where, as it turns out, their GP thought to call me, to see if I could help the situation to move along. I couldn't.

Without an acceptance from the client the mind won't play ball. However, there are a number of ways to get permission. If you've ever wondered how stage hypnosis works, it is very simple. If you are in the audience, then you have given your permission, otherwise you wouldn't be sitting there, right? Now, I've just finished that last sentence with a tag question 'right?'. A 'tag question' gets you to confirm what has been said, yes? You'll notice that you start nodding and agreeing with me, do you not? Once you start agreeing the neurochemistry inside the brain builds into an affirmative YES, which makes it almost impossible for us to say NO! I wonder if the corporations that run T.V and media networks know anything about influencing us without us knowing? Imagine if a No/My was on prime time television, nudge nudge, encouraging us to comply with lots of secret messages. I say 'imagine'; however the reality is the UK government have been deploying the Behavioural Insights team, known as the "Nudge Unit" since David Cameron in 2010[143], to impact the very fabric of our society[144]. Please be aware you have already given your permission; you just didn't know. That's how influence works.

I've always maintained that the client must be willing to help themselves and in this particular instance, the client most certainly was not. Lez still very much cared for his wife's wellbeing, he wished her well and wanted her to move on with her life. They had the finances to go their separate ways, but she didn't want to let him go. This unwillingness impacted

---

[143] https://www.instituteforgovernment.org.uk/explainers/nudge-unit#:~:text=What%20is%20the%20Nudge%20Unit,has%20operations%20across%20the%20world.

[144] Please download 'Mindspace' from the UK government website to discover first hand what our government has been doing to us without our knowledge. The model has also been sold to other countries. https://www.instituteforgovernment.org.uk/publications/mindspace

on Lez's level of happiness as he was always worrying about his wife's drinking.

When Elizabeth and I met, she was polite, but cautious, she had done some homework on me and was on her guard. This kind of client is just too much like hard work and the very reason why I no longer allow them access to me. Figuring that neither of us was comfortable in the situation I asked, "Can we cut to the chase?" Elizabeth nodded. "Why won't you divorce him?" This seemed like the only question worth asking and if we could get some leverage, well you never know. Elizabeth scowled at me and replied, "I'd rather he was unhappy with me than see him happy with somebody else." Wow! It doesn't come much more twisted and clearer than that. Elizabeth knew that her husband still loved her, but he wasn't in love with her. She was quite happy in the knowledge that her spite and morose demeanour was hurting him, at the cost of her own health.

When you play that rule back inside your mind does it sound happy, healthy or loving? Elizabeth had run their business with Power and her family were afraid of her. Lez had wanted to sell the business 7 years earlier, but Elizabeth would have none of it. She loved the prestige and the power that her role gave her, she was not about to abdicate her throne. It was around this time Lez met his new partner, she initially offered Lez a voice to talk to, this would eventually give him what he had been missing for years, love and self-worth. Lez (Your/.) had been driven into the ground by Elizabeth (No/My) but inch by inch he reclaimed his life. When he left the marital home 3 years earlier, he took nothing but his pride. He didn't expect that he would be leaving Elizabeth to drown inside a bottle, but he had been desperately treading water himself for years. This was her tragic, yet wonderful plan. She knew each day that she struggled would hurt him and she was steadfast in her decision.

The driver here could also have been 'Until death us do part' as Elizabeth was determined that she would never let her husband go. This is only conjecture, but a bitter, angry, resentful pain could also be driven by the same Family Rule. This would also explain why Elizabeth would not move on, with such a Family Rule in place, she could not move outside the parameters of the marriage vow. The marriage had died, there had been a death to allow them to part. All of this information was packed inside of me, I wanted to engage with her to connect to share, to help, but not this time. One session was all I was given, as I said Elizabeth hadn't asked for my help and the door to her mind was welded shut.

Behind every door is another story, social media and mainstream networks (MSN) offer up these insights on a near daily basis, as we observe on the surface two beautiful people getting married. It's the dream, the fairytale wedding. Let's see how it plays out in this next case study, which is totally fabricated as these patterns seldom come in for real help, owing to their need for the limelight.

TOO GOOD TO BE TRUE

Bianca-Caprice Jones, the beautiful girl next door has fallen in love with Tony Smith, a topflight football player. She now has the identity of a Wag, an acronym, which stands for wife and girlfriend of a famous athlete, especially a footballer. The couple have now been married for 2 years, have 2 children and Bianca-Caprice has had enough of her husband. She explains her pain to the press, Tony has been having affairs throughout their short marriage. It's a headline grabber as two kiss and tells sell their story to the same press agents. People with empty lives buy the magazines with the full inside story, otherwise known as gossip! If Bianca-Caprice divorces her husband she will get a £50 million divorce settlement, she can take the children away from the pain and raise them in a nice home. Does the mother of 2 take the cash, her self-worth, her darling children and start over or does she accept Tony's apology and 'try' again? Yes, you've guessed! She stays! This leaves us with another Family Rule, 'If you marry for money you'll end up earning every penny'.

Bianca-Caprice is now a 'someone', being married to a footballer. "Before becoming a wag" she explains "I was a no one". We could spend years deliberating her perceived identity, but remember, she hasn't come to us for help, she's come because it might add a few more paragraphs to next week's issue of her daily gossip column. She might even hold back for an exclusive.

The 'too good to be true' is a subset of a Family Rule, it's a limiting belief. The Family Rule underneath this will be seated around rejection, being rejected from the tribe means death. Maybe Bianca-Caprice could have left Tony before they were married, but now she is tied to 'until death us do part' and ultimately believing that without her lying, cheating husband, she will become a no one again. If you want to do some further research of your own on this particular pattern look up Katie Price and Peter Andre or Cheryl Tweedy and Ashley Cole or Coleen and Wayne Rooney.

SPRING CLEAN YOUR MIND

'Spring Clean Your Mind' is the article below, it was written by Christine Fieldhouse, a freelance journalist, after interviewing me for a feature in the Daily Express (UK Newspaper). As you read it you can see how a few adjustments helped Christine to rapidly upgrade her beliefs.

"First, Matt asked me to note down all the things my parents taught me about work, so I rack my brain for memories from 40 years ago. My late mum Margaret was my main influence and she had very strict rules. She told me to always do the very best I could; to work as hard as I could and if I say I'm going to do something, to do it, no matter what.

For every belief, we went through a process of writing down the rule, then saying it out loud to bring it into the present and my conscious mind. As I did, I could hear my mum's Yorkshire accent clearly and relived how I felt as a child when I heard those words. Sometimes I felt a determination to do my best and a desire to rise to the challenge but on other occasions I was overwhelmed at what I had to achieve.

Images appeared in my mind to show how I'd stored these rules in my mind over the years. I pictured a woman flogging a child to make her work hard and an old-fashioned schoolmarm speaking sternly, dressed in black and white. Neither happened to me – my mum was a wonderfully kind woman – but the associations of strictness were vivid.

Once my internal rules were unlocked and my feelings out in the open, Matt started "re-programming" me. Together we altered each belief to bring it up to date and in keeping with the person I am now, not the six year old I was. As soon as I read out a new rule, I knew instinctively if it was for me. An old belief such as "always do the best you can" became "I can only do the best I can when I can and that's OK".

Looking at friendships, I revealed how my mum insisted I should never tell friends any personal secrets. Working with Matt, I turned this into "I can tell my true friends what I want when I want."

When we looked at my attitude to intelligence, the beliefs of my late father Harry came flooding back to me. According to him, I was clever but I would always need to work hard; I had no common sense and men wouldn't think I was very bright.

All of these statements evoked memories of sadness, desperation and a fear of intelligent men. As we worked through them, I realised why I'm happier dealing with women and how I'm much more confident when I'm doing talks about my writing to women only groups.

Meanwhile, my attitude to being a mother threw up some very old-fashioned legacies, including a belief that women who have children don't have much money. My mum told me this when I was a child – it was probably true in the Sixties when few mothers worked – and I'd held onto this belief and applied it when I became a mum. After playing around with the statement we rewrote it to become: "I have a child and I can make money when I want," which made me feel much more in control.

After leaving the session I felt in transit between the old and the new me. I figured I might believe the new rules for a day or so, and then I'd probably slip back to the old ones. Matt didn't agree: "Take a computer that's been updated from Windows 95 to XP. If it's upgraded, it remains upgraded. The mind is like that too," he said.

Since then, I've stood up for myself more, probably because I no longer see myself as a little girl trying to do her very best to please everyone.

By changing just a few core beliefs I've finally moved from the Sixties to the 21st century. Now I'm working on the next generation by drip-feeding Jack with my new, modern set of rules. Sometimes I slip in a sneaky one to ensure I'm looked after in later years. Well, sons should treat their elderly mothers to luxurious holidays, shouldn't they?"[145]

It is possible to change core beliefs, however, they can still be held in place by a Family Rule, which is why I took to writing this book. You and I have seen how easily the mind can be influenced, yes? The difficult part is knowing which parts of reality we have chosen, from the parts that we have been nudged into. Our next chapter should give us enough ammunition to arm ourselves against those No/My's who wish us to be subservient Your/.'s for the rest of our lives.

Chapter Summary

There are lots of rules within the family that can be upgraded easily, however, specific Family Rules can be very difficult to upgrade ourselves.

Family Rules can go beyond the boundaries of specific contexts.

---

[145] Fieldhouse C. Spring clean your mind. *Daily Express*. https://www.express.co.uk/life-style/health/41305/Spring-clean-your-mind. Published April 14, 2008. Accessed October 3, 2022.

9

A SOVEREIGN BEING

"Our deepest fear is not that we are inadequate.
Our deepest fear is that we are powerful beyond measure.
It is our light, not our darkness that most frightens us.
We ask ourselves, 'Who am I to be brilliant,
gorgeous, talented, fabulous?'
Actually, who are you not to be?
You are a child of God. Your playing small does not serve the world.
There's nothing enlightened about shrinking, so that
other people won't feel insecure around you.
We are all meant to shine, as children do.
We were born to make manifest the glory of God that is within us.
It's not just in some of us; it's in everyone.
And as we let our own light shine, we unconsciously
give other people permission to do the same.
As we're liberated from our own fear, our
presence automatically liberates others."
Marianne Williamson[146]

This final chapter has been whirling around inside my mind for the past month for many reasons. I have prevented myself from beginning; now it is time. A curious mind has driven you

---

[146] *A Return to Love: Reflections on the Principles of "A Course in Miracles"* .

and I through these pages, we are both seekers of knowledge, lifelong learners. The next sequence is an assumption, I have a hypothesis and I want you to test it for me in your life. My hypothesis:

"A sovereign man or woman will live a happier, healthier, longer life, and be in harmony with the planet".

This will no doubt take many years to come to fruition, however, it's the hill that I will die on. When we check the history books we can see poor mental and physical health has been around forever. This will be a subject for another book, but for now please take a look at John Sarno M.D's book *'The Divided Mind - The epidemic of Mindbody Disorders'*. Sarno reminds us that "psychosomatic medicine specifically refers to physical disorders of the mindbody, disorders that may appear to be purely physical, but which have their origin in unconscious emotions, a very different and extremely important medical matter"[147].

The frustrations that we face as we go through life create mountains or molehills for us, depending on how we observed our parents dealing with similar issues. As children these experiences then influence our likes, dislikes, desires and yearnings. As Adler informed us in Chapter 2, the roles that we are born into e.g., son, daughter, brother, sister and also the birthing order, may contribute to who we eventually become. When John Bowlby, the British psychiatric researcher, published *Attachment*, he explored the relationship effects between parents with their children and personality development. He wrote "The reversal of roles between child, or adolescent, and

---

[147] https://www.wob.com/en-gb/books/john-e-sarno/divid-ed-mind/9780715637272?gclid=CjwKCAjws--ZBhAXEiwAv-RN-L3GWetuyrisyJogLcwTWisiZ23o4sKEVP4VMyrX5WBMZ3DCak-dJc_BoCCscQAvD_BwE#GOR001336966

parent, unless very temporary, is almost always not a sign of pathology in the parent," he added "but a cause of it in the child"[148]. Renowned addiction expert, speaker and author Dr. Gabor Maté who is sought after for his expertise on trauma, addiction, stress and childhood development tells us "Role reversal with a parent skews the child's relationship with the whole world. It is a potent source of later psychological and physical illness because it predisposes to stress."[149]

Our work into Split-second Unlearning has shone light onto the speed at which these traumatic experiences (great or small) can effectively be released, let go and unlearned in a moment. The visual field had been our target until recently, however this book has taken a different course; we are searching for words, phrases or statements that may be triggering the auditory amygdala. As we have learnt, Family Rules are auditory based and it's conceivable to think that they will not be transformed by interrupting an eye movement. We need specific dialogue to be as concise and direct as when tracking a visual emotional memory image, but for the auditory track.

WHAT DOES YOUR ROLE MEAN TO YOU?

We are all playing roles as we go through life, but how much do we really know about the drivers behind the part we are performing? If I asked you to write down what 'Father' means to you, then asked you to do the same for 'Mother' you may find yourself writing about the parent you did or did not have! If you are married and have a husband, wife or civil partner,

---

[148] John Bowlby, *Attachment*, 2nd ed. (New York: Basic Books, 1982). 377.
[149] Maté Gabor. (2019). 13. *When the body says no: The cost of Hidden Stress* (p. 172). essay, Ebury Digital.

what does that mean? What does it mean to be a husband, wife or civil partner?

Adam, was 30 years old, still living with his Dad and had never had a girlfriend. I asked him to finish the sentence "I am ……..." he replied, "I am Adam", "I am a son", "I am a brother", "I am loyal", "I am faithful", "I am single", "I am sad", "I am frustrated", "I am lonely", "I am stuck". If you try those identity roles on for a moment what do you notice? Feeling inspired? I didn't think so. This was the top-level identity that Adam was running, and you can bet every eligible female would run a mile if he tried to advance on them (which he wouldn't).

Now, I would like you to guess based on what you have read above, what my next question was? I'll fill in the next few seconds with a reminder that Plato said, "Let no one, however rich, or noble, or fair, persuade you to give him the cure, without the charm."[150] I was about to administer 'the charm' in order for Adam's mind to accept 'the cure' within the very construct in which Plato has left us.

Times up! My next question, which is elementary if we follow all that we have learned so far…, "When did your parents split up?" Adam's face flushed red. "I was 10" he said, as his eyes filled. I then proceeded to unpick Adam's identity roles, so he could consciously follow the irrational cause of his irrational problem. His mother had cheated on his father, how do we know? He said "I am faithful" meaning if I ever have a relationship I will never be unfaithful. He also said "I am a son" therefore he was loyal, (to his father in this case as his mother had cheated), he held a below conscious grudge towards her, even though it wasn't his to hold. It was Adam's father who was angry, poor little Adam was just sad, he had lost his mum.

---

[150] https://pages.ucsd.edu/~dkjordan/arch/greeks/PlatoCharmides.html

If we overlay systems theory to this event, Adam's father created a closed system with his family and shut his children off from mentioning their mother. Systems theory shows the level of sensitivity a system has to its external environment, if it's open it will be responsive to change, if it's closed it will be insensitive to environmental deviations[151]. With this view we can begin to see more clearly how Adam is unable to create a loving relationship with a partner, consciously he is ready and willing to create an open system, however his subconscious mind has its learned experiences embedded in a closed system. This explains why Adam didn't say "I am a boy", he didn't need to! It oozed out of every cell in his body, which would shoo away any eligible female.

There was an EMI standing between Adam and the rest of his life; we were about to clear it. By the way in clock time Adam and I were now 10 minutes into our session and his closed system was about to begin the process of opening up. Can you sense the conflict taking place inside his mind. His father loves him and doesn't want him to get hurt by a woman the way he had been, but that's his father's reality, not Adam's. Dr Sarno explained this as a '*Psychosomatic Triad*', three "powerful unconscious realities that often work together to produce a psychosomatic episode"[152]. He explains them as "1. Deep feelings of inferiority. 2. Narcissism. 3. Strong dependency needs" (ibid p.118). Now, we don't know if Adam's father was narcissistic towards his son, but we definitely do know that

---

[151] Mele, C., Pels, J., & Polese, F. (2010). A Brief Review of Systems Theories and Their Managerial Applications. Service Science, 2(1-2), 126–135. https://doi.org/10.1287/SERV.2.1_2.126

[152] https://www.wob.com/en-gb/books/john-e-sarno/divided-mind/9780715637272?gclid=CjwKCAjws--ZBhAXEiwAv-RN-L3GWetuyrisyJogLcwTWisiZ23o4sKEVP4VMyrX5WBMZ3DCak-dJc_BoCCscQAvD_BwE#GOR001336966

Adam has inferiority and dependency problems, based on the identity roles he supplied.

After applying this process to clients over the years, I have devised certain short cuts which one might expect. John Mordecai Gottman, an American psychologist, Professor Emeritus of Psychology at the University of Washington, whose work focuses on divorce prediction and marital stability through relationship analyses, would sit through hours of watching couples argue before defining his work within the parameters of a split-second. The years Gottman invested in observing couples and predicting if they would divorce, culminated into his Cascade Model of Relational Dissolution[153] where he proposes criticism, defensiveness, stonewalling and contempt as key predictors of divorce.

He found that couples can have their arguments, their ups and downs and this was normal within a healthy relationship, however, if one of the couples showed any of the four destructive emotional reactions towards the other, the relationship would never last.

Adam's father had never re-married or even considered opening his life up to the excitement of having another relationship. We can extrapolate this from our interaction with Adam. We can then suggest that the *'narcissism'* could have definitely been present on a below conscious level, driven by Adam's father toward his mother and Adam was subconsciously picking up on this. At any rate, I'm pretty sure by now, that you are able to see the wider and deeper ramifications of Family rules, they are everywhere and nowhere.

---

[153] Gottman, J. M., & Levenson, R. W. (1999). What predicts change in marital interaction over time? A study of alternative models. *Family process*, *38*(2), 143-158.

THE SHORT CUT

The short cut in defining if a person is trapped inside a Family Rule comes down to one identity, which is specific to a male or a female. If I asked Erica to finish the sentence "I am…" and she responds with "I am a mother" then I can fill in the following ones for her, these will be Daughter, Wife, Sister, Caring, Aunt, Kind, blah, blah, blah! What's missing in Erica's identity is the same thing that was missing in Adam's. If I ask Erica what does wife mean to you? She will say loyal, sharing, caring, supporting, loving, etc, and the same would apply to a male who had written this as a husband. But what is missing?

Abraham Maslow spoke of our hierarchy of needs[154] (see the diagram below). Now, ask yourself which identity is missing for Adam and Erica? Here's a clue: It's the same identity that Kiranjit Ahluwalia and Sally Challen realised in the moment they snapped! The 'Snap!' is not actually a metaphor, it's the sound the rope makes as the elephant breaks free of her/his self-limiting beliefs. It's the moment when the slave (Your/.) says to the slave master (NO/My) enough! No one can hand this to you, you have to step up and take it for yourself, and I promise you a whole new world when you rise and shine. The identity of **Man** and **Woman** are ours by birth right, given to us by the creator of our universe, no one can stand above us, as we are one, together. The moment that you realise this fact is the moment that your life will change.

[154] McLeod, S. (2007). Maslow's hierarchy of needs. *Simply psychology*, 1(1-18).

Maslow's Hierarchy of Needs

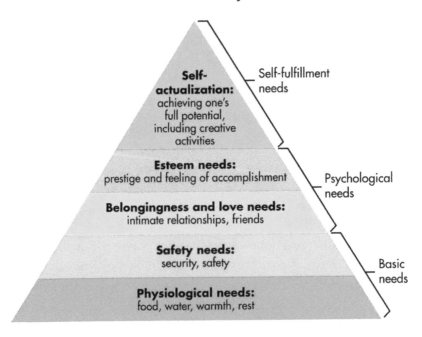

The No/My totalitarian rulers within our families have enforced their will upon humanity for generations, but now it is time. Time to say enough! The fundamental reason that I have found for psychophysiological dis-ease sits inside the mind of us all. If we are deprived of our basic human rights we shrink, we become compliant, hoping that those who harm us will stop; they never will, not until we take a stand!

What I've come to realise is similar to American Integrative Paediatrician, Dr Paul Thomas. Dr Thomas realised that he knew more about the vaccinated children than the unvaccinated, because the vaccinated children were always back and forward to his office for various treatments; the unvaccinated were not. To answer his conundrum, he applied science and published an extensive, peer reviewed, ten year study comparing the health outcomes of vaccinated versus unvaccinated children in his paediatric practice[155]. The difference in health outcomes was unconscionable.

In a very similar way, I was able to see that the people who I have helped over my career have all been missing the **Man** or **Woman** identity. **Man** and **Woman** are not roles, they are the trump cards, self-actualisation. The oppressed spirit kicks out and it is the body which suffers. From a scientific viewpoint the autoimmune system is unable to differentiate between the self and non-self, creating an internal conflict. A civil war, which can end at the moment the spirit of independence rallies the other 37.2 trillion single cells to rise and say "Enough!".

Think about your family and friends, how many of them are **Men** and **Women**? Not many. Yes, it can be tough making your own decisions and living a responsible life, but the good news is that you will enjoy optimum health whilst living a longer and happier life. Men and women have the ability to step in and out of Power or Achievement, whenever they wish, because they know who they are. They know what they want and do not need a No/My authority figure to tell them otherwise. Real men and women are not made of plastic, and you won't find them on the television. Why? Because they don't need the trappings that have been

---

[155] Lyons-Weiler, J., & Thomas, P. (2020). Relative Incidence of Office Visits and Cumulative Rates of Billed Diagnoses Along the Axis of Vaccination. *International journal of environmental research and public health, 17*(22), 8674. https://doi.org/10.3390/ijerph17228674 (Retraction published Int J Environ Res Public Health. 2021 Jul 22;18(15):) Yes the study was retracted by the journal but not for any scientific reason please read the retraction here: https://jameslyonsweiler. com/2021/07/25/mdpis-the-international-journal-of-environmental-research-and-public-health-does-not-publish-unbiased-research-or-advances-in-methodology/

offered for the purchase of their soul. They are not for sale and hopefully you my friend will step into the light of this new world too. We will welcome you, with open arms, hearts and one mind.

Conclusion

*"I'm not scared of the Maos and the Stalins and the Hitlers.
I'm scared of the thousands of millions of people that
hallucinate them to be "authority", and so do their bidding,
and pay for their empires, and carry out their orders.
I don't care if there's one looney with a stupid moustache. He's
not a threat if the people do not believe in "authority"."*
Larken Rose

Well, we've made it to the end of this particular adventure and with any luck a whole new sense of you and how important your being you, a man or a woman, will help to drive your quest for truth. Let's take a look at the road we have travelled and the themes that have come forth from the nothing, to make something out of our time together. I've had a few breakthroughs as I've drawn this information from my experience and the supporting evidence. If you have travelled with me up to this point, then I am deeply humbled that you have found the time to let me into your universe.

The various case studies can show the power of the Family Rules the subconscious prison that many are unaware of being trapped inside. Although I had been aware of the influence of the media, it wasn't until March 2020 that it really hit me. As a hypnotherapist, I witnessed a systematic trance induction being played out on the general public. As I said at the beginning of our journey, I have been putting off writing this book for years, the main reason being I didn't want to point to Nazi Germany to demonstrate the power of the No/My pattern in creating the Your/. compliance pattern. Then came the onslaught of totalitarian rule, not just from the UK government but by many other governments across the globe. Now, I had all of the ammunition I needed to support the Your/. claim and you, dear reader, have unravelled this with me.

The overwhelming amount of illogical information being spouted by supposed scientists and doctors stresses the system, making it difficult for us to make logical decisions. Just two weeks to flatten the curve, we all thought what is two weeks, so we complied, We are still continuing the 2 + 2 = 5 propaganda, even today I've witnessed first hand poor unfortunate souls walking outside wearing their symbols of oppression (the face mask). The government are very happy with the results of their labour, yet we the family, the children, are suffering.

I never expected to be reading books that have studied the doctors and medics in Nazi Germany in order to complete this book on Family Rules. Yet, with the current world view the work of Lidz becomes very poignant; eerily accurate. I was obviously naive enough to believe in the beginning, that real science and the light of truth would stop this psychological operation on mankind from proliferating, before others got hurt. I was wrong. It now appears as more and more dots are joined up, the environment is right for good people to do bad things. We could never have conceived it happening to us. The family, the children have born witness to many human rights violations, and it is here that I draw the line. The mice experiments tell us trauma can last at least four generations; we are working hard to raise awareness of Split-second Unlearning and the speed at which we can clear fear.

Bringing an end to fear for all is such a worthwhile cause that we created a free workbook to support this book. I want to help YOU uncover your OWN family rules, freeing your mind from rules or rulers who no longer serve you. Your freedom begins right here! Simply go to my website, https://matthudson. com/family-rules-okay/ to receive your complimentary, and very practical, guide to self-discovery. You will see for yourself that 2 + 2 really does = 4.

In the new world there will be a Great Reset but not the one that is being pushed by Klaus Schwab and the World Economic Forum. A world where the family comes first, where the parents are free from psychological attack and children can be happy learners, free from the confines of the Draconian education system. We have allowed this to happen, yes they have manipulated us, but now it is time, time for us to awaken, time to rise and shine.

"The winter of totalitarianism gives way to a new spring of life"
Mattias Desmet

If you take the blue pill you can finish this book and continue your life as it was. If you take the red pill then you can choose to wake up and see the world for what it is. A homogenised life that is served to you daily. It's time to join the millions of others who have cried "Enough!" and begin your real life.

To access your free workbook, and many more additional resources, go to https://matthudson.com/family-rules-okay/ and enter the password 'riseandshine'. The consequences of taking no action may well be the difference between life and death. So, what are you going to do now? This really is "do or die." Are you ready to free your mind? Are you curious? Realise there will never be a right time and leap into the abyss, with the knowledge that you can, and you will rise and shine!